YOUTH AND COMMUNISM

Youth
and
Communism

An Historical Analysis of International
Communist Youth Movements

Richard Cornell
State University of New York, Buffalo

WALKER AND COMPANY · NEW YORK

16730

Author's Note

To Professor Alexander Dallin and Mr. Robert Bass goes my sincerest gratitude for making it possible for me to do this study. To many individuals and organizations who contributed their time and gave of their knowledge go my thanks for assistance. Specific mention must be made of Mr. William Ellis, Mrs. Elizabeth Marbury Bass, and two officers of the United States National Student Association, Mr. Alexander Korns (International Affairs Vice-President) and Mr. Frank Crump (Director, International Student Visitor Service). Needless to say, no one but myself should be held accountable for the interpretations made, or errors committed.

Contents

Introduction

In recent years student-led movements have threatened and toppled a number of governments, forced the cancellation of a visit to Japan by the President of the United States, and influenced, often violently, developments in many crucial areas of the world. Students were the first to demonstrate in opposition to the Diem government's repression of its Buddhist opponents; students were instrumental in fomenting the uprising against Syngman Rhee in South Korea in April 1960, and even today are emerging as South Korea's most powerful pressure group; in Burma an unrelenting student campaign of agitation against the government has been under way for some time; university students in Venezuela and elsewhere throughout Latin America have been active in pro-Castro agitation and violence; in France the students at the Sorbonne have demonstrated in protest against inadequate higher education facilities; in the United States young people, white and Negro, have been active in the campaign for equal rights; and in the Communist countries of Eastern Europe young people in general and students in particular have openly expressed their dissatisfaction with

Communism. Behind this increase in student initiative lies the dissatisfaction of the younger generation with the pace of progress toward improved educational opportunities, economic betterment, and, in many cases, political freedom. The growing influence of youth, most particularly in the developing countries, and its impatience with the wide gap between reality and ideal, provide a fertile field for radical slogans and programs.

The interest of the Communist movement in young people is nothing new. It has been evident ever since the Bolsheviks acquired power in Russia in 1917, and even before, and is the logical outcome of the totalitarian nature of Communism. The considerable effort devoted to organizing, indoctrinating, and controlling youth has been one of the more notable attributes of all modern totalitarian societies. Although totalitarian regimes have taken steps to organize and control, in one degree or another, almost all activities within the state, their efforts in this regard with respect to youth have been particularly important. This held true for the pre-World War II Nazi and fascist regimes, and is evident today in the practices of states governed by Communist parties.

One need not look beyond youth itself in order to understand the reasons why totalitarian systems have been so concerned with youth activities. Young people are passing through a stage in human development in which new experiences and new relationships assume great importance. Youth, searching for something to adhere to, has not as yet committed itself. Youth is a period of intellectual and physical change—a time of trial and error in which the urge to explore and to satisfy natural curiosities leads the young person to seek to discover himself and his role in the world. It is a period of questioning, often highly romanticized, in which ideals of great purity and clarity often come to dominate the intellectual and emotional approach to life's problems, before maturity brings reality into sharper focus. It is also a period in which every question must have an answer. An exuberance that demands freedom from restraint in order to assure self-expression is one of the unique characteristics of youth. The result of this independence and self-assertiveness is that by nature young people are more radical with respect to the *status quo* than are adults, and less willing to accept authority.

On the one hand, therefore, the nature of young people provides totalitarian movements with ready-made ground upon which to sow their complete, simplistic, and often idealistic dogmas. By appealing to the nobler aspects of youth's aspirations with easy answers to the political and social problems of the day, and by taking advantage of youth's willingness to experiment and accept change, totalitarian movements have had considerable success in winning support from youth for their attacks on existing institutions.

On the other hand, a totalitarian movement once in power finds youth's independence and willingness to experiment a serious disadvantage. Steps must now be taken to direct this exuberance into channels useful to those wielding the instruments of power. A system that is mobilizing a society in its entirety to achieve some stated objective, and that permits no other objectives to be sought, or any means to be employed in reaching the stated objective other than those decided upon by those in power, cannot allow young people free rein to seek their individual places in the sun. Youthful exuberance and idealism are to be harnessed to regime-defined goals, and are not to be manifested in individual self-expression.

Against this ideological background, one must distinguish between the activities of the Communists among youth in those countries where Communists are in power, and their activities in countries where they are struggling to acquire power. On the one hand there are the Communist youth organizations established to further Communist objectives where the party is in power. In such countries, with all of the instruments of power under Communist control, the parties can take steps to organize youth as they see fit. All the Communist parties now in control of nation-states have taken steps to organize youth as one of their first tasks after assuming power.

On the other hand are Communist activities in countries where they are not in power, or are even proscribed. In many cases those Communists in power have prepared the way for the organization of youth by forming Communist youth groups in the period before the assumption of power. These usually form the nucleus of the mass organizations created after the Communists take control. Where the Communists are out of power, they are able to win support only to the degree that their appeals fall on receptive ears. Thus, organizing youth into Communist youth organizations becomes a matter of persuasion rather than of government directive. Where a free market place for opinions and ideas exists, the Communists must compete for adherents on the basis of their program. The approach to youth outside the Communist world, therefore, has been rather different from that within the bloc.

COMMUNISTS IN POWER

The essential attitude that Communist leaders have taken, once in power, toward youth is perhaps summed up best in the new program of the Communist Party of the Soviet Union adopted at the Twenty-second Party Congress in October 1961: "The Party regards youth as a constructive, creative force in the Soviet people's struggle for Communism."[1] The program goes on to call upon the Communist youth organization (Komsomol) to inculcate in youth:

> ...a spirit of boundless devotion to the motherland, the people, the Communist Party and the causes of Communism, and a constant preparedness for labor for the good of society and for overcoming all difficulties, and to raise the general educational level and technical knowledge of young men and women.[2]

The clear implication of these statements is that youth is only an instrument to be utilized for a higher goal—the achievement of Communism. Youth is to be made into a servant of "the Communist Party and the causes of Communism," and is to be prepared to work, not in its own interest, but in the interest of society as a whole.

No mention is made in the party program of the needs, hopes, and aspirations of young people, or of the way in which the party or the Komsomol could best assist them in furthering their own ends, since in a Communist society youth may have no goals apart from those of the party. The objective is to build a Communist society, and all individuals and groups are mobilized to this end. The interests of the individual, or of any special segment of the population, can have value only to the extent that these interests are part of the collective interest.

The historical antecedents of this view of the role of youth go back not much further than the Russian revolutions of 1917. Before that the leader and grand theoretician of the Bolshevik party—Lenin—had little to say about youth, or its problems. In fact there were only three significant references to youth by Lenin in the pre-revolutionary period. The second congress of the Russian Social Democratic Labor Party in 1903 (which preceded the split into Bolshevik and Menshevik parties) approved Lenin's resolution supporting independent revolutionary activity among students.[3] In 1905, Lenin called on the party to recruit more young people, because he saw in youth the most energetic and enthusiastic element in society.[4] In 1916, Lenin felt free to say that the attitude of the Bolsheviks toward those youths who were "vigorous, turbulent, and inquiring, but who lacked theoretical clarity," e.g. the radical youth who did not see things the way Lenin did, should be different from that toward adults who displayed the same "fault."[5] Patience was to be shown toward radical youths since they were active in tearing down the old and would in time be won over to Lenin's views on building up the new society. Such tolerance, however, was soon to disappear, once the Bolsheviks took power.

In the period of political uncertainty and growing tension after the February 1917 revolution, the Bolsheviks began for the first time to take a serious interest in youth. They called for radical improvements in the working conditions and educational opportunities for young workers. *Pravda*, the Party organ, carried numerous articles criticizing the Provisional Government for its inability to improve the lot of the young workers and peasants. Another issue that the Bolsheviks utilized related to the franchise.[6] The Provisional Government had proposed lowering the voting age to twenty, but only the Bolsheviks wanted it reduced to eighteen. Since the young were more willing than other age groups to accept radical changes, the Bolsheviks wanted the voting age as low as possible. They used the pages of *Pravda* to publicize their position, and to call on young people to struggle for political rights. The ability of the Bolsheviks to exploit legitimate grievances and aspirations by promising their complete fulfillment, immediately, was a key element in their successful assumption of power, and the support that they won from youth by their espousal of the most radical positions was of considerable importance in this regard.

After its victory, the new Bolshevik regime became extremely interested in youth; not because it was concerned with its grievances, but rather because it wished to consolidate itself in power. "After the October [November] Revolution, the whole attention of the [Bolshevik-inspired] youth leagues was concentrated on strengthening the dictatorship of the proletariat and defending it from the international and Russian counterrevolution."[7] A Communist youth organization (Komsomol) was formed within which there was considerable pressure in the early years (1918-1920) for genuine action in defense of the interests of youth. This "opposition," however, was soon eliminated. Instead, the Komsomol was given the task of organizing youth to aid in the efforts at increasing the productivity of the economy.

In 1920, Lenin laid down the guidelines of party policy toward youth, which have remained substantially unchanged ever since. Speaking before the third all-Russian congress of the Komsomol, Lenin called upon youth in general, and young Communists in particular, to educate themselves so as to be able to build the Communist society upon the foundation laid by himself and his colleagues.[8] Youth had to be trained to build a Soviet society. It had to *learn*! The masses of young workers and peasants, together with all other segments of the population, had to become instruments for carrying out party tasks.

From this beginning, Communists in power have carried on their youth work on two levels. On the one hand, among youth at large, Communist leaders have attempted, quite successfully, to educate in order to develop the skilled personnel necessary to build and operate a modern industrial society. They have also sought, with considerably less success, to impose sufficient discipline so that youth will turn with full vigor to the tasks set by the party. Alongside these efforts among the youth at large, the party leaders have utilized the Komsomol as a training ground for new recruits for the party.

COMMUNISTS OUT OF POWER

Of equal importance to the Communist movement has been work among youth in areas where Communists are not in power. Unable to exercise political control, Communists outside the Soviet Union prior to World War II could hardly take steps to organize youth for the purpose of "building Communism." Communist youth organizations could, however, serve the interests of the Soviet state. With the world balance of power clearly weighted against the Soviet Union, all international Communist organizations played an important role as auxiliary arms of Soviet foreign policy. Among these organizations was the Communist Youth International. In addition, national Communist youth organizations served as reservoirs and training schools for new recruits to individual Communist parties.

Communist international activities since World War II, including work among youth, have been directed toward objectives essentially similar to those in the pre-war period. The manner and means of this work have changed, however, in order to adapt Communist efforts to changed conditions. New organizations—the World Federation of Democratic Youth (WFDY) and the International Union of Students (IUS)—were created at the end of the war, and the illusion was fostered that these Communist-dominated organizations represented all the youth and students of the world.

Since the death of Stalin in 1953, fresh changes in front organization policy have appeared. In the developing countries Soviet policy under Khrushchev emphasized working where possible through the nationalist youth and student movements in order to influence them in favor of Soviet objectives, or win them outright for Communism. With the international Communist movement no longer displaying the monolithic traits of earlier times, however, one can no longer speak of a single Communist policy. Both the Soviet Union and Communist China have international youth and student policies, which are becoming increasingly divergent. Recent developments give evidence of a future split of the international Communist youth and student movements into pro-Soviet and pro-Chinese organizations.

Certain similarities do exist between youth organizations organized by the Communists outside the bloc and those inside. Youth in both cases remains an instrument of the Party. "Front organizations" directly or indirectly work to further the objectives set by the Communist parties. These Communist-sponsored or supported youth bodies remain reservoirs of potential recruits for the Party —whether pro-Soviet or pro-Chinese. Finally, the international Communist youth and student organizations are today, as they were in the pre-World War II period, rather obvious servants of Soviet (or Chinese) foreign policy.

The persistence of the view that youth is only an instrument of party policy, to be marshaled in pursuit of one goal, defined by that party, has often brought the party into conflict with the interests and desires of youth. In order to understand the role youth has played within the Communist movement, it is necessary to study Communist youth in action by tracing its growth within the Soviet Union and outside and to discuss the successive shifts in Communist tactics toward youth. It will also be helpful to analyze the problems that Communist leaders have had to face in making youth receptive to their appeal and to evaluate the degree to which they have been successful in fulfilling their objectives. What follows is therefore a description and analysis of the Communist youth movement as it has unfolded over the years.

1/Chapter
The Birth of the Communist Youth Movement (1915 — 1925)

The origins of the Communist youth movement lie not in the Soviet Union, but in Western Europe. The Communist youth organization formed in the new Soviet state after the Bolshevik revolution of November 1917 was the first in name only. It was an organization with very limited historical antecedents since the labor and Socialist movement in pre-revolutionary Russia had been strictly controlled by the Tsarist regime. The activities of political organizations other than those of the Right were severely circumscribed, and this was particularly true of any efforts to organize youth. The activities of the Bolsheviks in the area of youth affairs in the years before 1917 were thus quite limited, and confined almost completely to student circles. In Western Europe, however, the situation was quite different. Here the Socialist youth movement had been functioning since before the turn of the century. The revolutionary Socialist youth organizations were products of the long process of political development that the Socialist movement in general had undergone.

The international Socialist movement, centered in

Central and Western Europe, contained from its beginning a number of diverse groups differing on matters of doctrine and tactics. Although there was overlapping between different points of view, and divisions within each, the Socialist movement gradually came to be divided into three main tendencies—Right, Center, and Left. Orthodox Marxism held that in order to free itself from the "shackles of capitalism" the proletariat had to overthrow capitalist society by revolution. In the late nineteenth century a Right wing developed within the Socialist movement that questioned the necessity for such revolutionary tactics. Taking a second look at the capitalist society that Marx had criticized, it concluded that Marx should be revised to take into account the possibility of attaining socialism through democratic procedures. This Right wing came to be known as the "revisionists" or "reformists." The orthodox Marxists opposed revisionism, but soon were divided into two factions. The Left, in which Lenin and the Russian Bolsheviks played a predominant role, remained uncompromising revolutionaries. A group that came to be known as the Centrists stood between the Right and the Left. It condemned revisionism and espoused revolution, but stood against the violent assumption of power by a minority as advocated by the Left. To the Centrists, revolution meant any change that removed the capitalists from power and put the proletariat into power, a change that they foresaw as coming after a long process of development, and that would in all likelihood see the proletariat in a majority. Emphasizing democratic procedures, the Centrists ceased in practice to be active revolutionaries. It was from the Left that the Communist parties, and the Communist International, emerged in Europe and elsewhere in the years after World War I. Inevitably these political divisions in the international Socialist movement came also to be reflected in the international Socialist youth movement. The course of developments within the Socialist youth movement, however, was somewhat different from that within the Socialist parties.

The formation of Socialist youth organizations began in the late nineteenth century.[1] The first such organization was founded in Belgium in 1886. Its main function was to conduct anti-militarist propaganda among the young soldiers being used against strikers and demonstrating workers. Other groups of this type followed in Sweden (1895), Switzerland (1900), Italy (1901), Norway (1902), Spain (1903), and the south of Germany (1904). Still other Socialist youth groups were formed in Austria-Hungary (1894) and northern Germany (1904-5) primarily to fight for improvements in the deplorable working conditions of apprentices and young workers. In some cases these youth organizations had been formed independently of the Socialist parties, but usually with party support; in other cases the parties founded the youth organizations themselves and kept them under their control.

In 1889 the Second International was founded at a congress in Paris of representatives of Socialist parties, but it was not until 1907 that an international union of Socialist youth organizations was formed at a congress in Stuttgart, Germany. The International Union of Socialist Youth Organizations (IUSYO) was a loose federation, primarily oriented toward the education of young workers in the principles of socialism and the theory of class struggle. Of secondary importance were anti-militarist propaganda and efforts to improve the living and working conditions of young workers. The youth international was an independent organization, although its leadership worked closely with the Second International. Nevertheless it, as well as national Socialist youth organizations, was kept out of the factional controversies between Right, Center, and Left within the Second International, and was looked upon by the latter as well as by its own leadership as primarily a "recruiting school" for social democracy.

This policy of keeping youth out of political affairs had its critics. Those youth organizations that were independent of the Socialist parties (primarily in Scandinavia and Italy) were leaders in a developing movement to foster a stronger, more politically active youth international. Opposition to the policy of keeping youth out of politics also existed in the party-controlled German, French, and Swiss Socialist youth organizations. The "opposition" groups in these countries were mostly influenced by Leftist or Centrist elements within the Socialist movement, and were thus highly critical of the lack of revolutionary emphasis that dominated the thinking of these Socialist parties. Being strongly against war, and hostile to imperialist rivalries among the European powers, the proponents of an independent, political youth international were united by the emotionally charged issue of anti-militarism. They wanted the youth international to be free to carry out a vigorous anti-militarist, anti-war, and anti-capitalist campaign.

With the outbreak of war in 1914, the international Socialist movement broke apart, as did the youth movement. The Right-wing Socialists, who were in a clear majority within the Socialist parties in the belligerent countries, except in Italy and Russia, for the most part supported their respective national war efforts. The Centrists and Leftists vigorously opposed the war, but where the Left violently denounced the Right as "social patriots" and worked for the creation of a new, actively revolutionary Third International, the Center sought to maintain the unity of the Socialist movement. Center and Left joined in an anti-war "opposition" within the Socialist movement, but the differences between them over the path to revolution, and the tactics to be followed, made for an unsteady alliance. The Left advocated turning the war into a revolutionary "civil war between the classes," and sought to commit the Centrists to the principle of violent revolution. The Centrists, however, were basically pacifistic, as well as being in a majority within the "opposition," and thus rejected the tactics of the Left and supported all efforts to end the war, even if it meant leaving the capitalists in power.

Lenin and the other Bolshevik exiles constituted perhaps the most important segment of the Left, and after the revolution in Russia their prestige rose considerably.

With the end of the war in November 1918 the uneasy coalition of forces in the "opposition" broke down. The conflicts in the international Socialist movement came to a head, and a split occurred. Once in power in Russia, the Bolsheviks took steps in early 1919 to capitalize on the general climate of crisis and political tension and moved to form a new, Communist International.

SOCIALIST YOUTH AND THE WAR

Developments in the international Socialist youth movement during the war generally followed those within the parties.[2] There was an important difference, however, which was to be of great significance after the war. The leading body of the Second International (the International Socialist Bureau) had, shortly after the outbreak of war, passed into the hands of neutral Dutch Socialists, who, together with the Scandinavian Socialists, attempted to get the Socialist parties of the belligerent countries together with a view toward ending the war. Those in charge of what was left of the Second International were mostly Right Socialists, and thus anything but revolutionary. The leadership of the youth international, however, passed not only into the hands of the anti-war "opposition" in 1915, but into the hands of those who had by the end of the war fully come to support the revolutionary views of the Left.

As in the Socialist parties, there was a division of opinion among the Socialist youth over the war effort. The Socialist youth organization in Germany, by far the largest and best organized, had never belonged to the youth international. As it was subordinated to the Social Democratic party, it gave its support to the Right Socialists, and hence to the war effort. French Socialist youth likewise accepted the decision of their Socialist party to support the war. The Austrian youth organization, however, quickly changed its initial expression of support and came out in complete opposition to the war. In Britain there was no Socialist youth organization to speak of. In Russia, also, there was no Socialist youth organization. Instead, the younger Russian exile Socialists were active in party affairs, and did not form a separate youth group. Support among the Socialist youth for the policies of the Left in general, and the Bolsheviks in particular, had to come, therefore, from among the youth of Western Europe.

The leaders of the anti-war "opposition" in the Socialist youth movement were the Socialist youth organizations in the neutral countries. The most active force in rallying anti-war Socialist youth and in guiding the affairs of the youth international during the war was the secretary of the Swiss Social Democratic youth organization, Willi Münzenberg, who enjoyed the support of the three Scandinavian Socialist youth organizations.

The career of Willi Münzenberg makes an interesting story.[3] He was a young German who had drifted to Switzerland in pursuit of better opportunities. He became active in the budding Socialist youth movement in Zurich, becoming the leader of the Swiss Social Democratic youth organization in early 1914. In this capacity, he became associated with Lenin, Zinoviev, Radek, and other Bolsheviks in exile in Switzerland. In November 1917 he was arrested by the Swiss authorities for publishing inflammatory materials and participating in demonstrations. Released in March 1918, he was rearrested the following May, and finally expelled to Germany as an undesirable alien after the end of the war. Immediately he became active in the Leftist "Spartakus" movement, which in December 1918 provided the nucleus for the Communist Party of Germany (KPD). He was arrested by the German authorities in January 1919 for participating in the revolutionary events of that month, and was not released until June. Until its second congress in Moscow in the summer of 1921, Münzenberg was the leader of the Communist Youth International (CYI), as well as an active participant in the affairs of the KPD.

The anti-war "opposition" in the youth international succeeded in reviving the organization at a conference in

Bern, Switzerland, in April 1915,[4] that adopted a new constitution and reorganized the international along new
lines. The result was that the International Union of
Socialist Youth Organizations, set up as an independent
political organization with the International Youth
Bureau, now the executive body of IUSYO, transferred
from Vienna to Zurich, and Willi Münzenberg as the new
International Secretary. The manifesto adopted by the
conference called for an immediate end to the war, and
declared it to be the duty of all Socialist youth to support
the efforts for peace then under way within the international Socialist movement. Despite the efforts of Lenin
and the Bolsheviks, the conference did not adopt the
radical program of the Left. For the most part, the Bern
conference was looked upon as a demonstration of international Socialist solidarity and anti-war feeling.

The reorganized youth international quickly gathered
support, and by the end of the war all of the existing
Socialist youth organizations except the German, French,
and Dutch had joined. It published a quarterly in German,
Jugend-Internationale (Youth International), which
became an important forum for the anti-war "opposition."
Jugend-Internationale was distributed illegally in Germany, where it became a link between the various "opposition" party and youth groups. Articles were translated
into the Scandinavian languages and reprinted in the
national Socialist youth press in those countries. Another
important activity of the youth international was the series
of International Youth Days that the International Youth
Bureau sponsored in the fall of each year, during which
demonstrations, rallies, meetings, and speeches were
utilized to arouse youth in all countries against the war.
Understandably, these activities were more successful in
the neutral countries, where restrictions were not nearly
so severe as in the belligerent states.

Nevertheless the predominant influence in the youth
international during 1915 and 1916 remained with the
Centrists, and the organization continued to support the
policy of seeking unity in the Socialist movement. The

objective was to end the war, while preserving the Socialist movement as a force capable of influencing the peace that would follow. As the war went on, however, a process of gradual radicalization took place. Members of the International Youth Bureau and most member organizations of the youth international came to support the actively revolutionary position of the Left. This turn to the Left was the result of many factors. Horror at the carnage on the battlefield and weariness with hardships brought on by the war combined to produce a more revolutionary mood in most of the European countries. Youth in particular, as the prime source of manpower for the trenches, rapidly developed an anti-war attitude. Socialist youth was also frustrated at the apparent inability of the Socialist parties to bring about an end to the war. The Bolshevik revolution in 1917 became for many Socialist youths a symbol of the end of "capitalist exploitation" and "imperialist wars." Having less at stake in the old society, youth was more willing to accept the radical policies of the Left.

Yet at no time did Socialist and other much smaller youth movements on the political left (syndicalist, anarchist) encompass a majority of the young people in any country. In many countries the Socialists were unable to organize a significant portion even of working-class youth, their most logical source of support. In the prewar years, youth had remained for the most part under the influence of religious and other non-political youth movements, such as the Boy Scouts. During the war, the large majority of youths in the belligerent countries rallied to the national war effort. The youth international thus succeeded in winning over a majority of Socialist youth for a revolutionary policy only in the neutral countries.

THE BIRTH OF THE COMMUNIST YOUTH INTERNATIONAL

The end of the war in November 1918 and the formation of the Communist International (Comintern) in

March 1919 found the Socialist youth international in existence, but rather disorganized. Revolutionary unrest in Central Europe, as well as the continuation of governmental controls on travel, made communications very difficult. Willi Münzenberg was in jail first in Switzerland and then in Germany for most of the time between November 1917 and June 1919; thus the continuity of leadership that he provided was absent at a critical time. It was in these circumstances that two parallel efforts were made in 1919 to convene an international Socialist youth conference.

In Switzerland, the International Secretariat was endeavoring to call a *general* conference in Vienna in August 1919. Meanwhile a small group, under the aegis of the Comintern, was planning a conference in Moscow composed only of clearly revolutionary youth organizations. This latter conference was to create a Communist Youth International, to work under the Comintern. The intention was to split the international Socialist youth movement, as the Comintern had already split the Socialist parties. However, when the overthrow of the Hungarian Soviet regime in August 1919 made it impossible to hold the Comintern-sponsored conference in Budapest, representatives of the new Russian youth organization agreed to merge their efforts with those of the International Secretariat.

A conference was finally held in Vienna at the end of August 1919, but it was far from a general international Socialist youth meeting. Travel difficulties restricted the attendance to representatives from the Russian Communist youth organization; the two working-class youth organizations in Austria—the old Social Democratic youth organization under Centrist influence, and the very small, newly formed Communist youth organization; the Left elements in the German "opposition" youth group (now split off from the old Social Democratic youth organization into a separate organization in which the Left predominated over the Center); Münzenberg and two others from the International Secretariat; and several supporters of the Russian Communists from the youth organizations in Poland and Hungary. Representatives of the Right-wing Socialist youth were not invited.

The majority at Vienna supported the Russian position, which favored the formation of a Communist youth international. A majority, however, over the opposition of the Russians, was also for inviting, not only the revolutionary Socialist youth on the Left, but the Centrist youth organizations as well. In the end, the Vienna conference formed a Provisional International Youth Bureau of five members, which was to prepare for another international conference in Berlin to include representatives from both the Left and the Center. It was also to function as the executive organ of the IUSYO until a permanent one was chosen at that conference. When, however, Münzenberg, who was a member of the Provisional Bureau, came out in support of the Russian position on the exclusion of the Centrists, a new majority was formed and the die cast for a conference of only those Socialist youth organizations that supported the Left, and for the formation of a Communist youth international.

During 1919 the factional controversies that raged in the Socialist parties were also at work within the Socialist youth organizations. The Communist International had been formed, and the Russian Bolsheviks were active in support of efforts to found Communist parties. By the time the international Socialist youth conference met in Berlin in November 1919, the Socialist youth organizations in Sweden, Norway, Denmark, Switzerland, and Italy had become supporters of the Left and an actively revolutionary program, and all supported the new Comintern. Outright Communist youth organizations had been formed in Russia, post-war Austria, Poland, and Hungary—all but the Russian organization being very small, with the latter two illegal and in exile. Very small revolutionary, Left youth organizations existed in Holland, Spain, Romania, and Czechoslovakia. The "opposition" youth organization in Germany (*Freie Sozialistische Jugend*—FSJ) had split, and the Left had expelled the Centrists. Thus three work-

ing-class youth organizations existed in Germany—a large
Right Socialist group that was rejuvenated after the war,
the small Centrist, and the growing FSJ, which supported
the new German Communist Party. The French Socialist
youth organization was still under the control of the Centrist French Socialist party, but the pro-Comintern faction, which was in 1921 to win control of the French
youth organization, was laying the basis for its rise to
power. In both the Czech and German areas of the new
Czechoslovakia, the Left was in a minority but growing
rapidly.

All of the revolutionary, Left Socialist youth organizations were represented at the Berlin conference in
November 1919 except the Dutch.[5] No Centrists attended.
The congress was treated by the participants as the first
regular congress of the IUSYO since before the war, despite
the fact that the Right Socialist and Centrist youth
groups—many of whom had been members of the IUSYO
—were not present.

The principal result of the Berlin congress was the
capture of the old Socialist youth international and its
transformation into the Communist Youth International,
which represented a sharp break with both the pre-war
and wartime youth internationals. From an organization
tied closely to the Socialist parties and predominantly
educational in character, the Socialist youth international
had moved continually during the war toward becoming
an independent revolutionary political movement. It did
not, however, take sides between the Left and the Center,
seeking rather to maintain unity in the Socialist movement. The new program adopted at Berlin gave firm support to the Bolsheviks and marked a clear break with all
other factions, thus aligning the youth international quite
clearly with the Left.

The Berlin congress was the culmination of efforts by
the Left to capture the youth international. Where, however, Lenin and the Left in the international Socialist
movement were forced, by their minority position and
their inability to capture the International Socialist

Bureau, to set up a new, Third International, the revolutionary youth was able to capture an existing organization. Several factors contributed to this. For one, the control of the executive body of the IUSYO before the war had been in the hands of those anti-war elements that came to be identified as Centrists. When, in order to keep the youth international functioning as a symbol of international Socialist solidarity during the war, this control was given up at the time of the Bern conference, the IUSYO was placed in the hands of the more radical and future Communist elements.

A second factor leading to the acquisition of control by the revolutionaries was the real support that the Bolsheviks in Russia and the new Third International enjoyed in the ranks of Socialist youth at this time. The Bolsheviks were admired for being the only successful revolutionary Socialist group, and there was much sympathy for the Comintern among Leftists no less than Centrists in Germany, Sweden, Norway, Italy, Spain, and Switzerland; support was also growing in France and Czechoslovakia.

Although the formation of the Communist Youth International marked the final split in the international Socialist youth movement, it was not the end of the conflict. The CYI promptly extended its work in various countries, seeking to consolidate the Communist position by destroying the Centrist groups, winning over their membership, and then challenging the Right Socialists for control over the young workers. The Communists made a sharp distinction between "real" revolutionaries (themselves) and the "traitors to the working class," by which were meant the Right Socialists and those Centrists who opposed unity with the Communists. The major areas of conflict were France, Germany, and Czechoslovakia. In France and Czechoslovakia the Communists succeeded in capturing the Socialist youth organizations and driving the Centrists out. In Germany, the small remaining Centrist youth organization was infiltrated and split, the majority affiliating with the Communist youth organization of Germany (KJD).

Thus, by the latter part of 1920, the Communist Youth International had won acceptance for its program from the organizations represented at the Berlin congress, and had for the most part succeeded in capturing or splitting the Centrist youth organizations. It was at this time, however, that the latent political differences between youth and adults, between the CYI and the Comintern, between the Western Europeans and the Russians, began to break the surface of unity.

In the early years of the Comintern, the young Communists in Western Europe were among the more uncompromisingly revolutionary elements in the Communist movement. This was particularly so of most members of the CYI Executive Committee (ECCYI). The young Communists were strong supporters in 1920 and 1921 of the "theory of the offensive," whose advocates in the various countries sought to bring about a Soviet system through revolutionary action by a dedicated minority. The founding of the Comintern in 1919 was, in fact, an expression of the belief that all that was needed to consummate the revolution was a truly revolutionary leadership to guide the supposedly revolutionary masses. And the European political situation in early 1919 was indeed one to give encouragement to such a view.

The "revolutionary offensive" was at its height in the period 1919 to 1921, and its main proponents were the leading figures in the Comintern—Zinoviev, Bukharin, Karl Radek, and Bela Kun. Not only had the Bolshevik leaders believed in November 1917 that the success of the Russian revolution would depend on revolution throughout Europe, but the intervention and Civil War in Russia during 1919 and 1920 spurred the Comintern leaders to take steps to foster that revolution.

The Soviet offensive into Poland in the summer of 1920 seemed to all Communists the occasion that would trigger the long-awaited European revolution. At the second Comintern congress, which took place at the height of the Soviet military offensive, Lenin called for the acceleration of "the revolution." When the Soviet offensive was checked, however, plans for spreading the revolution to the rest of Europe became hopeless. Advocacy of a "revolutionary offensive" was no longer tenable.

By the early spring of 1921 it was clear to Lenin and Trotsky that consolidation and temporary retreat were necessary. In domestic policy this meant the introduction of the New Economic Policy; in foreign affairs it required efforts to establish normal diplomatic and trade relations with the Western powers; in the Comintern it meant the abandonment of the "revolutionary offensive" and greater emphasis on gaining influence over the majority of the working class. The advocates of the "revolutionary offensive," however, were still as convinced as ever of the need for and possibility of revolutionary action.

THE SOVIETS AND THE CYI

The Bolshevik leaders, therefore, by means of the Comintern and the Russian Communist youth organization (Komsomol), moved to discipline the CYI and the Western European Communist youth groups in order to break up a strong source of support for the "revolutionary offensive" and assure "proper" Comintern and Russian control over the youth movement. Not only was it necessary to bring the Communist Youth International under Comintern control, but as the Russian party was now asserting its own control over the Comintern, so was it necessary for that party, through the Comintern and the Komsomol, to assert control over the youth movement.

The early assertion of an independent political line by the CYI had been made possible in part because Russian youth leaders had not been able to control or influence the Communist youth movement in Western Europe. At the Berlin congress in November 1919, the Russian representative had not been able to win acceptance of the program drafted in Moscow without several major modifications. After Berlin, the Komsomol was too busy with its own problems of organization during the Civil War to pay much attention to the Western European movement. In addition, the military and political situation was such as to make communication between Russia and the Western European countries extremely difficult. The Executive Committee of the CYI, led by Willi Münzenberg and supported by the largest and most influential Communist youth organization outside Russia, the German FSJ/KJD, therefore continued to lead the Communist youth movement in Europe.

With the end of the Civil War, however, the Komsomol leadership was able to devote its main energies to organizational problems, both within its own organization and within the international Communist youth movement. As the Komsomol attempted to assert itself as the dominant force within the CYI, a conflict began to develop between the Komsomol, the CYI Executive Committee, and the German Communist youth organization.

The disciplining effort that was now initiated by the Russian youth leaders, assisted by the Comintern leadership, was an expression of a more fundamental cleavage on basic principles, the most important of which involved the relationship of the Communist youth organizations to Communist parties. From the outset a difference of views had existed in the CYI on this issue. At the Berlin Congress, the Bolshevik view on complete unity and centralization had been presented by the Russian representative. After a lively debate, this concept carried the day insofar as the youth international was to be subordinated to, and not a "sister organization" of, the Comintern. A significant minority, however, remained unconvinced that the youth international should be subordinated to the Comintern and they found support among member youth organizations.

The decision on the relations between the Communist parties and the youth organizations at the Berlin Congress was a compromise—the youth groups retained their independence, but were obliged to maintain close contact with the Communist parties and to support their activities. After Berlin, however, the controversy over independence was continued within the youth organizations and in the pages of *Jugend-Internationale*.

Three distinct positions were discernible in the debate. At the one extreme were the proponents of absolute political autonomy. At the other were the Russian youth leaders, who advocated complete subordination of youth to the parties on the Russian model. In the middle, attempting to reconcile the need for central control and firm discipline in the Communist youth movement with the desire to avoid becoming merely an instrument of Russian policy, was the ECCYI and Münzenberg.

A long and spirited debate in CYI publications, as well as in the national Communist youth press, was carried on during the latter part of 1920 and the spring of 1921, until the controversy was settled for good in the summer of 1921 at the third Comintern and second CYI congresses in Moscow.[6] The Comintern congress halted the "revolutionary offensive" and adopted a policy of cautious retrenchment. Admitting that the Comintern had paid too little attention to youth, the Comintern congress also discussed the youth movement as a special item on the agenda. It passed a resolution to the effect that youth organizations should no longer be active participants in political affairs.[7] Youth organizations were now to devote their attention to gathering together young workers and educating them in the theories of Communism. Political subordination to the Communist parties was to govern relations between the youth organizations and those parties. The CYI congress that followed made it clear to the delegates that youth organizations must give up their independent involvement in political affairs, especially their advocacy of the "revolutionary offensive."

The opposition at the CYI congress formally submitted to discipline, but on returning home these delegates did little to put the new policies into effect. They were aided by disapproval of the new Comintern political line on the part, variously, of large segments of the central leadership, the membership at large, or both. In addition, there were also those who, bowing to Comintern discipline, had become converts to the new line only to return home to an organization that gave them less than full support. Despite these difficulties, the central leaderships of the national Communist youth organizations were able in most cases to win a majority for the new line at national congresses of their respective organizations.

The ECCYI was reorganized immediately after this CYI congress to bring it firmly under Comintern and Komsomol control. The transfer of the ECCYI from Berlin to Moscow, its larger size and new composition, the creation of a sub-bureau in Berlin, the reorganization of the Western European apparatus, and the reassignment of Münzenberg to other work all helped take the administration of the Communist Youth International out of the hands of the old leaders who had advocated independence, and to put the Comintern and Komsomol leaders in firm control.

Partially owing to this controversy over control, Communist youth organization membership declined during 1921-1922. Other significant causes for this drop included the generally negative reaction among young workers to Communist revolutionary activities in 1921, and a general ebbing of the revolutionary tide in Europe. Young people were simply more concerned with getting on with reconstruction and improving their standard of living than they were in attempts to overthrow the existing system.

The Right Socialists and the Communists went their separate ways. Centrist youth, left out of the Berlin congress despite its desire to participate, formed—at a meeting in Vienna in February 1921—an international that stood between the Communists on the one hand and the Right Socialists on the other. It considered both to be one-sided—the one completely political and a mere tool of the Communist parties and the Comintern; the other tied too closely to the reformism of the Right. When finally faced with definite Communist refusal to cooperate with them, the Centrists turned to the Right Socialists and merged with them in 1923 into a new Socialist Youth International that, if not in form, was in spirit the real successor to the pre-war IUSYO.

While the Right Socialist and Centrist youth internationals were moving toward unity during 1921-1922, the Communist Youth International was embarking on a "united front" policy. The Communists thus hoped to extend their influence among the young workers of the Right and Center and to become the largest and most influential among young workers' organizations. These "united front" efforts met with very little success, however, because of the patent insincerity of the Communist proposals.

Aside from attempts to create "united fronts" in the name of economic reforms, the CYI was also working to form "united fronts" in other fields. The Red Sports International (RSI) was created in July 1921. Sports groups being large and popular in most countries, the Communist tactic was to attempt to win control of them and to give them a subtle but definite political character. By making them successful they further hoped to extend their popularity, thus attracting youth of all, or no, political persuasions. Between 1922 and 1924 the RSI attempted to get the Socialist sports international to cooperate in joint sports events, but the latter resisted all Communist overtures.

The Communists were also quick to attempt to make use of university students in many countries. In some cases, young intellectuals provided the core of Communist youth organizations. Despite the normal receptivity of students to radical ideas, however, the Communists were at no time successful in winning a really sizable portion of students in any country.

The year 1923 was for the international Communist youth movement, as for the Communist movement as a whole, a period of intense political activity. Resistance to the Franco-Belgian occupation of the Ruhr resulted in an economic crisis in Germany, and gave rise to new Communist expectations. Communist youth, especially in

France and Germany, agitated within the national military forces. Clandestine publications were distributed to soldiers. Meetings and discussion groups were held where possible. All agitational efforts were keyed to the prevailing political situation and aimed at developing a revolutionary, "anti-capitalist" spirit among young soldiers. The Communists thus hoped to turn the recruits against the authorities by pressing for demands that they knew the authorities could not grant, including better pay, better living conditions, and relaxation of discipline.

Established as a political movement, the Communist Youth International in its early years was involved primarily in political activities. It was anxious to build up its own image, and preoccupied with the conflict among rival working-class youth movements, with relations between itself and the Comintern and between Communist parties and youth organizations, and with controversies over political tactics. There was little time left for efforts to assist young workers, and such assistance as was given was always a tactical move in support of some political goal, *never* an end in itself. Indeed, the Communists argued that the condition of the young workers could never be significantly improved under a capitalist system and that only the "proletarian revolution" would bring real improvement. Hence organizational and political problems took precedence almost by definition.

The great "victories" claimed by Communist youth in these years turned out to be rather hollow ones. The capture of the organization of the old Socialist youth international (IUSYO), the winning over of long-established Socialist youth organizations in some countries, and the capture of several large Centrist youth organizations did not result in a powerful Communist Youth International. The extremism of the Communists did not for long suit the mood of the European working class. Furthermore, the initial support or sympathy for the Bolsheviks within the labor and Socialist movement drained away rapidly as the repressive nature of the Russian "dictatorship of the proletariat" became more than the European

Socialists could accept. Almost everywhere Communist youth organizations became partisan groups clearly identified as the adjuncts of local Communist parties. Only in Sweden, and in Germany, were they able to retain a significant membership. By 1923, when the Socialist Youth International emerged from the union of Right and Centrist Socialists, the Communist Youth International had ceased to be a significant element in the Communist movement. It was in the new Soviet Russia that the Communist organizational techniques were to be first applied to youth.

THE ORGANIZATION OF RUSSIAN YOUTH

The formation of a Communist youth organization in Russia began in 1917.[8] With the overthrow of the monarchy in March, strict controls over political activity were lifted and all political factions began to engage in active organizational work. One by-product was that a great many youth organizations came into being. Some of these had a definite political affiliation, others were non-political. The most active organizing efforts were undertaken among young workers, and were concerned first and foremost with social, cultural, and recreational problems. The largest and most significant of these new youth groups was an organization in Petrograd called "Labor and Light." It was basically apolitical and attracted youth from all Leftist parties—Bolshevik, Menshevik, Socialist Revolutionary, and others. It was concerned primarily with improving the condition of the young worker.

After the March revolution, the Bolsheviks also turned their attention to youth. They concentrated their efforts in Petrograd and Moscow. In Petrograd they not only worked to undermine "Labor and Light" but built their own youth organization, called the Socialist Young Worker's League. Soon they were successful in acquiring a dominant influence over the more politically active young workers, and in August 1917 a conference of young workers' representatives agreed to dissolve "Labor and Light" and endorse the Socialist Young Worker's League. This new organization again contained young workers who supported all of the Leftist parties, and, while still concerned with the interests of youth, it soon became a definitely political organization, open to Bolshevik influence and manipulation.

The young workers' movement in Moscow developed along two lines from March to November 1917. The first Bolshevik youth group was the "Third International" Young Worker's League, formed shortly after the March revolution by younger supporters of a district committee of the Bolshevik party. Groups on the same model began to be formed in other districts in April, and by July the organization had grown to about 1000 members and had established nuclei in several factories. While it had a strong Bolshevik faction, the "Third International" organization was also constructed on a broader foundation, while a second, smaller youth organization was built on a strictly Bolshevik basis in July by the Moscow Committee of the Bolshevik party. This group, however, failed to win much influence among the masses of young workers, and was presently merged with the "Third International" group.

The Bolsheviks first discussed their official attitude toward youth at their party conference in Petrograd in July 1917. A youth organization directly under the party; a youth organization organizationally independent of the party, but under its control; and a mass organization of young workers free of party control were all discussed as possibilities. The sixth congress of the party in August once again discussed the youth issue and passed a resolution "On Youth Leagues." The congress advised local party organizations to give the most serious attention to the organization of youth, but this was *not* to lead to direct tutelage. The Bolsheviks realized that they were in a distinct minority within the Russian labor movement, and that any attempt to assert Bolshevik domination would drive away potential supporters. The objective of the Bolsheviks in Russia at this time was the same as that in

Western Europe—first to get youth out of the hands of the other Socialist parties, then to infiltrate the youth organizations and win them for the Bolsheviks. The party was to see that its youth organizations developed in the "proper way" and that they maintained their "spiritual bond." There was to be a tie to the International Youth Bureau, under Willi Münzenberg and the Leftists, and local party groups were to stress those themes that appealed to all youth, such as anti-militarism and the rights of youth. In this manner it was hoped that the class-consciousness of young workers would be developed, and that this in turn would lead to support for, or acceptance of, the Bolshevik program.

After the Bolshevik victory in November 1917 there was no immediate effort to gather all existing Bolshevik-oriented youth organizations into one central organization, or to break up the other existing youth organizations. The Bolshevik hold on the instruments of power was not yet firm, and they were above all concerned with consolidating their position.

By the fall of 1918, however, the party decided to form a centralized youth organization and thereby to divert restive youth into channels appropriate to Bolshevik purposes. The first all-Russian congress of young workers and peasants was convened in Moscow in late October and early November 1918 on the initiative of the Moscow "Third International" youth group and the Petrograd Socialist Young Worker's League. The 176 delegates, representing 22,100 members, were divided as follows: 88 Communists, 38 Communist sympathizers, 45 non-party, one Left Socialist Revolutionary, one anarchist, and three Social Democratic Internationalists. Whatever political independence the "Communist sympathizers" and "non-party" delegates may have enjoyed in theory, it is clear from the results that the congress was Communist-dominated. A new, all-Russian youth organization was formed, uniting those youth groups in which the Bolsheviks played the leading role. Yet while the new organization appears to have been the largest and best organized youth group at this time, it still represented a minority of all youth in Russia. The new organization was expected to make common cause with the Bolshevik party, and while retaining its independence, to work under party guidance. Thus the Communist youth movement from the outset was formed on the "front organization" principle, and only later, as Bolshevik control was more firmly established, was the guise of an independent youth organization dropped.

One disputed issue at the congress was whether or not to include the word "Communist" in the name of the new organization. Many feared that the term might alienate young people and especially peasant youth. The majority, however, supported inclusion of the word, and hence the organization became known as the Communist League of Youth (or Komsomol, from the abbreviation of the name in Russian).

THE KOMSOMOL

Soon after its founding, the Komsomol began to move against other existing youth organizations. The Boy Scouts were apparently prohibited in 1919, and toward the end of 1920 the Menshevik and anarchist youth organizations were broken up and their leaders arrested. Despite these steps, the Komsomol did not succeed in immediately eliminating all rival youth groups. Until the late 1920s, when Stalin consolidated his control over the party, organizations of young Jewish, Menshevik, Socialist Revolutionary, Christian, and Boy Scout groups managed to survive, usually in rural areas and in the Caucasus and the Far East.

During the Civil War of 1918 to 1920, Communist youth was active in the fighting. The Komsomol was used to mobilize young supporters of the Bolsheviks. In May 1919, and again in October, special recruitment drives were carried out, and several more were undertaken in 1920. Yet because the most loyal youths were needed for military assignments the organizing activities of the Komsomol were severely handicapped, and at the end of 1919 it remained a relatively small organization of about 100,000 members.

With the end of the Civil War and the conflict with Poland in 1920, the party turned with full vigor to the task of tightening control over its youth organization and defining the role that the Komsomol was to play in the new society. This process of imposing party control over the youth organization in these early years is of considerable interest, since it shows how the Komsomol was turned into one of the instruments by which the population as a whole was mobilized to fulfill the party program.

The course of party-youth organization relations closely followed the fortunes of the Bolsheviks. The more successful they were in asserting their power, the tighter grew the relationship between the party and the Komsomol.

At its inception the Komsomol was a relatively independent body, and the Bolsheviks relied largely on young party members to maintain control and keep the organization in line with party policies. Most of the key positions in the Komsomol were in the hands of these young party members, but the further down the chain of command one went the less firm that control became.

Shortly after the founding Komsomol congress in October 1918, the party sent a circular letter to all local organizations outlining the nature of the Komsomol and its relation to the party.[9] The letter stated that the Komsomol, while working with the party, was an independent organization. Uniting "the broad masses of the working youth in order to build them into a conscious army for Communism," the Komsomol was to: (1) struggle with the Communist Party for the attainment of Communism; (2) spread the ideas of Communism among young workers and peasants; (3) draw young workers and peasants into active political struggle under the banner of the Soviet revolution; and (4) defend their legal and economic interests. The letter recommended that all party members of the proper age enter the Komsomol and take an active part in its work.

At the eighth congress of the Communist Party in March 1919 the independence of the youth organization was stressed once again. "Communist work among youth can be successful only through independent organizations, advancing under the banner of Communism, in which youth is able to exercise the maximum degree of independence, which is absolutely necessary for its Communist education."[10] The party congress recognized the Komsomol as such an organization. It also stressed the importance of work among youth in order to provide "well-trained reserves" for the party. The congress called on the Komsomol to: (1) educate youth in Communism; (2) mobilize youth for the building of a Communist society; and (3) defend the new Soviet republic.

Shortly after this congress, however, a significant change occurred in the relationship between party and Komsomol. Following the advice of the Komsomol Central Committee (which consisted of leading supporters of the party in the youth organization), the party Central Committee in August 1919 issued a joint declaration with the Komsomol Central Committee "On the Relations of the Russian Communist Union of Youth and the Russian Communist Party (Bolshevik)."[11] The party activists in the Komsomol seem to have decided that a tighter rein on youth was necessary. No longer was the Komsomol referred to as independent—it became instead an "autonomous" organization working under the control of the party Central Committee and the local party committees. The Komsomol Central Committee was to be "directly subordinated" to the party Central Committee, and the local Komsomol organizations were to be under the control of the corresponding local party committees. All members of the party under twenty-one were obliged to enter the Komsomol. Where no youth organization existed, the party was to take steps to form one. The local party organizations were to establish factions within the local youth organizations when the latter: (1) followed a non-Communist line; (2) displayed weak political work; (3) were influenced by "petit bourgeois" elements;

or (4) had no party members in their governing bodies. Such factions were "to guide the active work of the youth organization in a Communist spirit." Yet despite this tightening of control the party was careful to take into account that it still needed to win the loyalty of the mass of young people. Warnings were issued that control of the Communist Party over the youth organization was not to lead to tutelage or petty intervention in the work of the Komsomol. Local party groups were not empowered to dissolve local Komsomol groups—all "misunderstandings" were to be resolved by higher party and Komsomol bodies. Finally, both the party and the youth organization were to give each other complete support and cooperation in each other's activities.

During 1920, as the Bolsheviks drove to a successful conclusion of the Civil War, the membership of the Komsomol rose steadily to some 400,000 members, and with this increase in numbers discipline became more of a problem and latent discontent within the Komsomol began to grow. There were those who began to chafe as the party moved to increase its control of Komsomol affairs. These elements urged wider rank-and-file participation in the determination of Komsomol policies. Also, some of the national Communist youth groups (particularly in the Ukraine) sought more local autonomy.

The leading dissidents, however, were soon removed from their Komsomol positions, an action ratified at the third Komsomol congress in October 1920, which also adopted a new program bringing the relationship of Komsomol to party into line with the joint declaration of August 1919. In accordance with the new program:

> The RCLY [Komsomol] acknowledges the program and tactics of the RCP [party]; in considering general questions of the life of the Soviet Republic, it [the RCLY] subordinates itself to its [the party's] political directives and, working under its [the party's] control, is an autonomous organization. The CC [Central Committee] of the RCLY is directly subordinate to the CC [Central Committee] of the RCP.[12]

Also, with the Civil War over, youth was no longer to concern itself with political affairs, since now the party no longer needed the support of youth in its political battles. What the party did need, however, was support in the giant task of reconstructing the economy. In order to increase farm and industrial production, the "New Economic Policy" (NEP) was introduced in 1921. The strict controls and forced requisitions of the Civil War period were abandoned in favor of limited free enterprise and private trade. In the absence of a trained pool of Communist technicians and managers, the government had to rely on holdovers from the old regime. To overcome this deficiency Lenin issued a call to all youth—Communist and non-Communist—"to learn!" The younger generation not only had to be molded into strong Communists, but had to be trained to take over the complex task of running the economy.

The youthful radicalism of the immediate post-revolutionary and Civil War days suffered a serious setback with the introduction of NEP. There was a serious drop in Komsomol membership and morale. The retrenchment policy of the regime appeared to the young radicals as an abandonment of Communism, and disillusionment was all the worse because youth was usually the first to suffer from job layoffs connected with the NEP drive for increased efficiency.

Concomitantly, the authorities encountered another problem that also resulted from the introduction of NEP. They became concerned lest tolerance of "bourgeois" economic practices might have harmful effects on their indoctrination activities. Hence the fourth and fifth Komsomol congresses in 1921 and 1922 were concerned with strengthening the "proletarian" nature of the organization and attempting to create a new sense of "proletarian morality." The use of tobacco and alcohol was not to be allowed, and sexual mores were to be tightened.[13] Steps were also taken to make it more difficult for those from other than a worker or peasant background to join the Komsomol.

The subordination of the Komsomol to the party and its assignment to non-political work was made even more explicit at the eleventh party congress in March-April 1922. There the view was expressed that:

> The Russian Young Communist League, being a mass organization for Communist education, serves the Party as a mighty weapon of Communist education and influence on the broad strata of young workers and peasants. At the same time, the Young Communist League, training within its ranks the most class-conscious and revolutionary part of the working youth, guarantees healthy and uninterrupted growth of the party from the most active strata of the proletariat—the young workers who come to the party through the League already trained for practical revolutionary work.[14]

Accordingly, the party undertook several practical measures to assure control of the Komsomol. The right to examine and approve the agendas of Komsomol congresses, increased control over the lists of candidates for election to Komsomol offices, and the introduction of restrictions on eligibility for holding Komsomol offices to those who had been active party workers were some of the measures introduced at this time. Another step had to do with extending control to younger children. Since the minimum age for Komsomol membership at that time was fourteen, local groups of "Young Pioneers" were to be formed under Komsomol guidance so as to teach children of ten to thirteen loyalty to the Communist Party. Although the Pioneers grew rapidly, by 1924 they still contained only a small portion of all Soviet children, and it was not until after World War II that they became a genuine mass organization. Sometime between mid-1924 and early 1926 an organization for children under Pioneer age was formed, called the "Little Octobrist" organization.

One result of the efforts to maintain the "proletarian" nature of the Komsomol in the NEP period was that young people became increasingly dependent on the Komsomol.

Improvements were made in their working conditions, some protection against unemployment was provided, and a system of factory schools was developed to enable young workers to improve their position. Thus membership in the Komsomol came to be a definite advantage, and by the spring of 1923 it had again risen from a low of about 200,000 in mid-1922 to some 400,000.[15] As had already been the case in 1920, this sudden influx of new members introduced "undisciplined" elements and again raised the problem of party control. Yet by 1923 the Komsomol had a sound footing and its rivals were virtually eliminated. It had extended its influence into the international Communist youth movement by acquiring control of the executive bodies and the administrative apparatus of the Communist Youth International. Although the Komsomol had been given an ostensible monopoly over youth affairs, the exercise of this monopoly was to be under constant and close party control. The NEP had done much to bolster the ravaged and devastated economy, and to ameliorate the harsh conditions of life. Yet, in fact, the trials and tribulations of the Komsomol were only beginning. All during 1923 Lenin lay ill, suffering from the effects of a stroke, and unable to exercise his leadership. The struggle within the Communist Party for power, which had begun during Lenin's illness, broke out into the open after his death in January 1924. The Komsomol could not avoid being caught up in this conflict.

2/Chapter
The Stalinization of the Communist
Youth Movement (1925 — 1941)

From the mid-1920s until World War II the international Communist youth movement was occupied primarily with tasks dictated by the Comintern in support
of Soviet foreign policy. Apart from its use as a source of
new recruits for the Communist parties, the Comintern
was interested in the Communist youth movement only to
the extent that it could further the Comintern's own
campaigns. The Communist Youth International was not
in this period, or indeed at any time, an organization
concerned with the basic problems of young people.

As a result of its clearly political and partisan character the Communist Youth International and its member
organizations mostly remained small and sectarian organizations during the 1920s and the early 1930s. They were
organizations of young Marxist revolutionaries and Soviet
sympathizers who were used by the Communist parties to
extend Communist influence among young people at
large. However, this close and clear identification of
Communist youth organizations with Communist parties
nullified for all practical purposes any efforts by the

Communists to extend their influence. They tended to attract only discontented, dispossessed, and inherently radical youth, augmented by some plain old naïve idealists. The only mass Communist youth organization was that in the Soviet Union. In most of the East European countries Communists, young and old, were prohibited, as authoritarian elements of the Right were either in power or in the process of acquiring power. In the Western European countries, the size and influence of Communist youth organizations diminished rapidly after the early post-World War I years of crisis and unrest. As economic stability and progress came to Europe, and as the authoritarian nature of the Soviet regime became more apparent, the radical positions of the Communists found a rapidly diminishing audience. Communist youth organizations suffered even more as youth sought other, more normal outlets such as sports and cultural and recreational activities.

In 1924 the total membership of the Communist youth organizations was only about 20 per cent of the also small Communist parties. By late summer of 1928 that figure had dropped to about 15 per cent.[1] While the German and Swedish Communists had some success in maintaining youth organizations of some size, the others did not. Complaints were voiced between 1928 and 1933 at numerous Executive Committee (ECCYI) sessions on the unsatisfactory growth of membership of the youth organizations.

PARTY CONTROVERSIES

An important element in the development of the whole Communist youth movement during the 1920s and early 1930s was its involvement in the struggle for power in the Soviet Union.[2] That struggle was one for control of the Communist Party, and through it for control of the new Soviet state. At the same time, within the Comintern, there was a conflict of policy on the strategy and tactics to be adopted to further the cause of world revolution. The two levels of the power struggle overlapped: the contending groups in the CPSU sought support from foreign Communist parties, while groups within the foreign parties sought to defend or attack one or another of the rival Russian groups to further or defend their own particular points of view.

The struggle over who would succeed Lenin emerged even as he lay on his death bed during 1923. Stalin, Zinoviev, and Kamenev joined to prevent Trotsky from assuming the leadership. Trotsky and the "triumvirate" were soon in conflict over the rights of opposition within the Party. Lenin, to whom any form of factionalism had become anathama, had had the party pass a resolution on unity in March 1921. Thus, when Trotsky attacked the new leadership by calling for criticism and more freedom for opposition in the Party, he was accused of violating Party unity and serving the interests of the enemies of the Party. In January 1925 the Central Committee took away Trotsky's primary source of power by removing him from the Commissariat of War.

Stalin, as General Secretary of the Party, then turned on Zinoviev and Kamenev and joined with Bukharin and others to form a new majority in the Central Committee. Meanwhile Stalin had been able also to extend his control to all Party organizations except that in Leningrad, which remained a Zinoviev stronghold. This Stalin-Zinoviev conflict came to a head at the Fourteenth Party Congress in December 1925 over the issue of "socialism in one country," which Stalin and his allies supported, and Zinoviev, Kamenev, and Trotsky condemned. The Congress gave overwhelming support to Stalin and his allies. During 1926 Stalin broke up the Leningrad Party organization. Zinoviev, Kamenev, and Trotsky were dropped from the all-important Politburo, although all still remained members of the Central Committee. In October 1927 Trotsky and Zinoviev were expelled from the Central Committee, and in November from the Party itself. Trotsky went into exile, and Zinoviev and Kamenev remained powerless.

The Comintern and the various national Communist parties also became arenas of conflict as a result of the power struggle within the Soviet Union. The youth organizations, however, only reflected a much paler image of the party struggle. Nevertheless the ECCYI and the individual youth organizations came out strongly against Trotsky because they were under the control of the Comintern and the Komsomol, both of which underwent a rapid process of "Bolshevization" as Stalin consolidated his hold over the Soviet Party and the international Communist movement.

The Fifth Congress of the Comintern in 1924 marked the beginning of this development. Having utilized undemocratic means to defeat Trotsky and his allies within the CPSU, Stalin now moved to bring the Comintern into line as well. Having initially joined forces with Zinoviev in order to defeat Trotsky, Stalin now sought to undermine Zinoviev's influence in the Comintern, of which he was the head and where he had developed considerable support. Two important factors contributed to Zinoviev's downfall. His defeat within the CPSU resulted in a serious loss of prestige and influence. Perhaps even more important was his support in 1924 of revolutionary activity at a time when no revolutionary situation existed. The resultant loss of strength in several of the Communist parties through premature violent action lowered Zinoviev's standing even further.

Inevitably, these developments affected the Communist Youth International as well. The formal subordination of the youth international to the Comintern had taken place at the Second CYI Congress in 1921, but much freedom of discussion had remained, and the national Communist youth organizations were by no means yet under the firm control of the Moscow leadership. The Fourth CYI Congress, however, following on the heels of the Fifth Comintern Congress, finally extended the decisions on "bolshevization" to the youth international. In September 1926 the leading supporter of Trotsky in the CYI, the Yugoslav Vujo Vuyovitch, was condemned

by the Presidium of the ECCYI for having utilized his
position as Secretary of the organization "to carry on
factional work against the unity of the Comintern."[3] He
was dismissed as Secretary of the CYI and suspended from
all CYI work. In October the Central Committee of the
CPSU removed Zinoviev from his position as head of the
Comintern and Trotsky from the Party Politburo. The
decision of the ECCYI Presidium to relieve Vuyovitch of
his CYI duties was upheld at the session of the enlarged
ECCYI in Moscow in November, when the Russian Komsomol representative took the lead in developing a solid
front for the Stalin-Bukharin majority in the CPSU and
the Comintern. All Trotsky and Zinoviev supporters in
the CYI were eliminated, while Stalin purged all elements
from the leadership of the Comintern that were not clearly
willing to follow the lead of the CPSU. A new leadership loyal to Stalin and Bukharin was formed when
Dmitri Manuilsky assumed active control of the
Comintern. Thus Stalin for the first time had his hands
directly on the Comintern apparatus, a grip that he was
never to relax.

In May 1927, when Stalin and Bukharin came under
attack in the Comintern for the failure of the United
Front policy, the Communist Youth International rallied
to their defense. The United Front policy of cooperation
with the Kuomintang and Chiang Kai-shek in China, and
the non-Communist trade unions in Great Britain, had
proved disastrous. In early 1927 Chiang turned on his
Communist allies and dissolved all Communist and left-
wing organizations in the areas under his control. In
Britain the collapse of the general strike in 1926 resulted
in the isolation of the Communists. Nevertheless the
ECCYI fully supported the Stalin-Bukharin-controlled
ECCI and their policies.

Moreover, the extent to which the CYI had, by this
time, become a tool of the Russian Komsomol and of
the Stalinist forces within the CPSU can be surmised from
the role that it now played during the showdown between
the Soviet First Secretary and his erstwhile ally, Bukharin.

The Stalin-Bukharin conflict was ostensibly fought on the issue of the peasantry's role in Russia's industrialization program, but it was in reality a struggle for political power. Bukharin had initially joined Stalin to oppose the rapid industrialization and collectivization policies advocated by Trotsky and Zinoviev, the defeated leaders of the so-called "left" opposition, only to discover that Stalin—once he had gained political ascendancy—was proceeding to adopt the platform of his routed opponents as a prelude to the introduction of the first Five-Year Plan. Denouncing Bukharin and his followers as a "Right Opposition" defending a reactionary peasantry, Stalin succeeded in having the Party Central Committee condemn Bukharin and his followers and remove him from his Party offices in April 1929. This included the leadership of the Comintern, a position Bukharin had held *pro forma* since the ouster of Zinoviev, even though in actual practice Manuilsky had been in charge.

During 1929 Bukharin's supporters still had some strength in the CYI, but little if any influence on the decisions of the ECCYI. In January 1929 the Presidium of the ECCYI supported the Open Letter of the ECCI on the "Right danger,"[4] and the CYI Secretary, the Russian Rafail Khitarov, had in fact participated in the ECCI discussions on this issue. The Presidium of the ECCYI called on all Communist youth organizations to support the Open Letter, and "to conduct a decisive and ruthless struggle against all Right and conciliatory groupings and tendencies in all Communist Parties and Young Communist Leagues."[5] In November 1930 the Presidium of the ECCYI condemned the union of the Right (Bukharin) and Left (Zinoviev) oppositions in the U.S.S.R.[6] The Russian and other youth leaders of both the Left and the Right were condemned, and the expulsions of Oppositionists from the Russian party were fully supported as evidence that Stalin had succeeded in establishing firm control over the CPSU, the Comintern, and the Communist Youth International. His followers were in leading positions in all of these bodies, and members of the

Oppositions had either recanted, left the Communist movement, or been expelled.

THE KOMSOMOL AS AN INSTRUMENT OF PARTY AND STATE

These party controversies obviously also had important repercussions on the Komsomol.[7] Many members of the Komsomol, including several on the Central Committee, supported Trotsky, some because they agreed with his more radical views, others because they opposed the curtailment of discussion and democratic procedures within the Party and the Komsomol. This opposition was an important reason why the annual congress called for by Komsomol statutes was not held in 1923. Instead in January 1924 the Komsomol Central Committee followed the Party line and condemned both Trotsky and his supporters in the Komsomol. The Central Committee also condemned another "deviation" that had arisen within the Komsomol, where many had chosen to remain neutral in the Party struggle. It was now made clear that this too was unacceptable and that the Komsomol had to come out in active support of the dominant "triumvirate."

During 1925 and 1926 the Komsomol reflected the clash between the Zinoviev-Kamenev Opposition and Stalin's new majority. Support for Zinoviev in the Leningrad Komsomol organization led to an attack on this group at the Seventh Komsomol Congress in March 1926, a few months after Stalin had triumphed at the Party Congress. Yet during 1926 the Party Opposition still had some success in seeking support from Komsomol members. A number of groups supporting Trotsky were formed, especially among students. These condemned the development of an authoritarian bureaucracy within the Komsomol, and asserted that Party control was stifling the youth organization. The only result, however, was the purge of thousands of Trotskyites from the Komsomol.

During the years 1926-1928 the Komsomol was so caught up in the effort to counter the Zinoviev-Trotsky

Opposition that it was able to accomplish little in the way of practical work. It did remain active, however, in the political education of its members, and in the work of the soviets, the trade unions, and other public organizations.

In one area the Komsomol was particularly active in support of Stalin's policy. Where Stalin saw the Party as only a workers' organization, the youth organization was to be both a workers' *and* a peasants' league. The Komsomol was, to Stalin, a "voluntary, free organization of revolutionary elements of the worker and peasant youth."[8] An important reason for this stress on rural youth was the weakness of the Party in these areas. Although the Komsomol also continued to be weak among the young peasants, it was often the case that a local Komsomol organization existed in a rural area, but no corresponding Party group. In these instances the Komsomol became the primary channel of Party influence. This, however, presented a problem with respect to control over these local Komsomol groups, now growing in size as more young peasants were recruited. Many of these new members were "middle peasants" who were not in sympathy with, in fact often quite hostile to, the regime's agricultural policies. Not only did the total membership of the Komsomol rise from about 200,000 in 1922 to 1,750,000 in 1926, but the number of rural members grew from 300,000 at the time of the Sixth Congress to 900,000 at the end of 1925.[9]

In 1928 the Communist Party terminated the New Economic Policy and embarked on the program of rapid industrialization under the Five-Year Plans. Stalin, now in effective control of the country, succeeded in putting the radical program he had taken over from Trotsky and the Left Opposition into practice: the pace was to be rapid and the burden was to fall most heavily on the peasantry.

With the introduction of the First Five-Year Plan and of forced collectivization, Party control over all organizations was tightened, as Stalin began to impose his personal dictatorship. The Komsomol was no exception. Many followers of Bukharin, especially among the recently enrolled rural members, were expelled, while criticism and discussion within the Komsomol became almost non-existent.

On the whole, however, the youth organization responded with fervor to the introduction of the Five-Year Plan. Here was something upon which youthful idealism could fasten. Thus the Komsomol organizations became the source of many mobilization drives to fulfill industrial and agricultural targets. As the Party had used members of the Komsomol during the Civil War for military tasks, so now they were utilized on the "industrial front." This was the beginning of a long tradition by which the Komsomol provides a large reservoir of manpower for special economic undertakings. The Stalingrad tractor factory, the Dnepropetrovsk electric power combine, new factories and lumber camps in the Urals and Siberia, the coal mines of the Donbas, and the Moscow subway were but a few of the industrial enterprises for which the Komsomol provided an important source of manpower. Young Communists were also sent into rural areas to establish collective farms (*kolkhozi*) and machine-tractor stations (MTS), and to help erase illiteracy and conduct anti-religious propaganda.

Meanwhile, Komsomol membership continued to grow—from 1,750,000 in March 1926 to 1,960,000 in May 1928 to 2,897,000 on July 1, 1930, and to 3,000,000 by the beginning of 1931. The Komsomol became the leading element in the move for increased "socialist competition." Production contests were organized by local Komsomol groups, as were competitions for best industrial workers. Komsomol organizations arranged "rationalization" meetings, at which means of improving the efficiency of enterprises were discussed. Members of the Komsomol were encouraged to become "shock workers," or workers who consistently overfulfilled their production quotas.

Military training of Komsomol members, made a formal obligation in 1921, also received increased emphasis at this time. During 1927 a serious "war scare" developed within the Soviet Union, and for the next several years the official Communist position was that the Soviet Union was in imminent danger of attack. Hence *Komsomoltsy* were to be ready to rise at any moment in defense of the "first proletarian State."

By the mid-1930s this initial blush of enthusiasm among young Communists had worn off. Continuous forced effort with little reward brought on disillusionment. Furthermore, the harsh measures taken to force the peasants into collective farms had serious repercussions within the Komsomol. Despite the many expulsions and "overhauls" of the Komsomol leadership, the size of the organization had increased by about 25 per cent between 1931 and 1936. These combined factors led to a radical reorientation of the Komsomol during 1936.

Important changes in the program and membership policy of the Komsomol were made at the Tenth Komsomol Congress in April of that year. Economic tasks were downgraded and emphasis placed on political indoctrination. The Party also changed the membership base of the Komsomol. Previously considered a mass "proletarian" organization, which recruited its members among young workers and poor peasants, the new program emphasized not social origin but loyalty to the regime as the essential requirement for membership. The Komsomol was to be a mass non-party organization, affiliated with the Party.[10] These measures resulted in a rapid growth in membership, which by the fall of 1939 had reached 9 million.

The Tenth Komsomol Congress also revealed the complete control that Stalin now exercised over the youth organization. Freedom of discussion and dissent, which had been on the wane for some time, was now effectively eliminated altogether. The professional youth leaders, or "activists," were in complete charge, and all initiative from below was gone.

The great Soviet purges of the late thirties inevitably affected the Komsomol. Denunciations and expulsions decimated the top leadership, as the Komsomol was caught up in the same reign of terror that swept through the Party.

After March 1939 and the Eighteenth Party Congress, the economic activities of the Komsomol returned to the place of predominance they had occupied prior to 1936. The Party again indicated that the Komsomol was to be an "active helper of the Party in all state and economic construction. Komsomol organizations must be in fact active conveyors of Party directives in all fields of socialist construction, especially where there are no Party organizations."[11]

During World War II, the military obligations of Komsomol members were paramount. The Komsomol mobilized the young people—with patriotic and nationalist appeals, rather than Bolshevik ideological slogans—to defend the country and defeat the enemy. Despite many defections, in no small measure due to the purges of the late thirties, youth rallied to the regime. Komsomol members were active in the front lines, with the partisans, and in the war production effort. The Komsomol grew very large during the war, apparently reaching a peak of 15 million members in the fall of 1945.

YOUTH AND THE COMINTERN

During these years, Communist youth leaders outside the Soviet Union directed the efforts of the Communist Youth International and national Communist youth organizations in support of the Comintern. The two most important areas of activity in the latter half of the twenties and throughout the thirties were the "struggle against imperialist war and militarism" and the formation of a Popular Front with the Social Democrats and other opponents of the new Nazi regime in Germany.

The CYI supported the Comintern view of world events in the late twenties, which held that there was a serious danger of a capitalist attack on the Soviet Union. The work of the CYI at this time concentrated on the "struggle against war danger and militarism, on the defense of the Soviet Union, and the revolutionary movements of the colonies and semi-colonies."[12] The anti-militarist policy of the youth international had been set in 1924 at the Fourth CYI Congress. It condemned pacifism and supported the policy that Lenin had long advocated of turning an "imperialist war" into an international civil war. It also made the work of Communist youth organizations among military forces a more important part of their general work. The hope was to establish organizational bases in the military forces, and to sharpen awareness among soldiers and sailors of their attachment to the working class. The application of this policy to the contemporary international situation took place in June 1925 when a conference of representatives of the European Communist youth organizations, called in the aftermath of the Western intervention in China and the French military action against the Riffs in Morocco, followed the Comintern view that a new phase of "imperialist wars" was opening. The conference decided to intensify the work in the armies so as to be able to turn such "imperialist wars" into a civil war against the national bourgeoisie.[13] It decided further to adopt a line of "active material and moral support of the national liberation movements in the colonial countries in order to defeat the imperialist governments."[14]

Numerous "campaigns" were also conducted by the Communist Youth International and its member organizations in furtherance of Comintern policies. In 1927, as relations between the Soviet Union and Great Britain grew more strained, and as the situation in China grew more serious, the official Comintern line was that the danger of a general war was becoming more acute. In March therefore the ECCYI undertook an "international week" against the danger of war, and against intervention in China and the Soviet Union. "Hands Off China!" "Down With Intervention!" "Immediate Recalling of All Troops and Battleships" "Against Imperialist Preparations for War Against the Soviet Union" were some of the slogans of this campaign. The Communist youth organizations other than the British, French, and Italian, however, did very little about this campaign. In June 1927 a joint manifesto of the British and Russian Communist youth organizations was published on the occasion of the British break in diplomatic relations with the Soviet Union. In August 1927, on the thirteenth anniversary of the outbreak of World War I, large demonstrations were organized by Communist youth in nearly all countries. The CYI also carried out a number of "jubilee" campaigns, using the tenth anniversary of the Bern youth conference (1915), the twentieth anniversary of the existence of the youth international (Stuttgart congress, 1907), and the tenth anniversary of the Red Army (1917) as occasions for concerted propaganda drives. Annual events of this nature included the Lenin-Liebknecht-Luxembourg Week in January, the anniversary of the Paris Commune (1871), and the anniversary of the Bolshevik revolution in Russia.

In November 1927 a Youth Conference of Friends of the Soviet Union was organized in Moscow from among delegations of young workers and youth that had been brought to the Soviet Union for propaganda purposes. The objective was again to mobilize support for the Soviet Union against "imperialist preparations for war." The delegates were expected to return to their countries and work for the CYI line. At the Fifth CYI Congress in 1928, Bukharin reiterated to the delegates the war danger facing the U.S.S.R., as did the CYI Secretary, Rafail Khitarov.[15]

UNITED FRONT AND "FRONTS"

Also very significant were the activities at that time of Communist youth in support of the Comintern's United Front campaigns.[16] Before 1924 the Communists had sought joint action with the Socialists through negotiations with leaders of the Socialist parties and trade unions. Then, furious at Socialist unwillingness to join in the revolutionary attempt in Germany in the fall of 1923, the Comintern abruptly rejected all further negotiations with Social Democratic leaders and subjected the Socialists to a virulent cascade of denunciations that lasted until after Hitler's rise to power in 1933. In this context a policy of "United Front from below" was launched in 1924, which sought to win members of the Socialist organizations away from their leaders by agitation among the membership at large and the formation of joint action committees at the local level.

Several different lines of action were pursued by the Communist youth organizations in attempting to carry out this new policy. There was the technique of the Open Letter, by which the Executive Committee of the CYI appealed to Socialist youth to join in common actions. These appeals appeared in the pages of the Communist youth press, and were also circulated as handbills and posted on walls in or near factories and other centers where young workers gathered. One such Open Letter was directed to the Second Congress of the Socialist Youth International in Amsterdam in May 1926, when the Communists called on Socialist youth to support:

1. Joint action against the "capitalist attacks" on the working class, and for better conditions for young workers.
2. Joint action against imperialism and the danger of a new "imperialist war."
3. The organization of young workers' delegations to the Soviet Union.
4. A joint defense organization of young workers in order to protect them against reaction, fascism, and the persecution of working class youth.[17]

A second element in the United Front efforts of the Communist Youth International was the attempt to penetrate and win over the youth sections in non-Communist trade unions. Despite considerable effort, however, especially in Germany, the Communists remained without meaningful influence in the mass working-class organizations.

A third United Front activity was the sponsorship of visits by delegations of young workers and other youths to the Soviet Union. By encouraging such trips by non-Communist, but sympathetic, young people, and by carefully organizing the itineraries, the CYI sought to establish islands of influence within non-Communist organizations. This program was started through an Open Letter from the Central Committee of the Komsomol to "young workers of all countries" in April 1926.[18]

A final means employed to win wider support among Socialist and non-party youth was the device of forming "unity committees." Wherever young people were active —in factories, schools, sports organizations, and elsewhere —young Communists were to take the lead in forming committees to work for specific objectives. These young Communists were to guide and direct the work of these committees, which were not, however, to be openly Communist. The call to these efforts was issued by a leader of the Comintern, the Finn Otto Kuusinen, in a report made to the ECCI in March 1926:

> The first part of our task is *to build up, not only Communist organizations, but other organizations as well*, above all mass organizations sympathizing with our aims, and able to aid us for special purposes .... We must create *a whole solar system of organizations and smaller committees around the Communist Party*, so to speak, smaller organizations working actually under the influence of our party ....[19]

Here is the beginning of the modern-day "front organization." The bodies that Kuusinen had in mind at this time were only the "unity committees," but the principle remained to be exploited later in other areas and on a much larger scale.

Actually the "front" activities of the Comintern had already begun during the early 1920s under the guiding hand of Willi Münzenberg, who had organized a food relief campaign in Western Europe after the end of the Civil War from which later sprang a whole network of "front" organizations that existed in the pre-World War II period.

These fronts, however, were not of importance for the youth movement. The first front activity that did involve youth was the League Against Imperialism, formed under Münzenberg's guidance at a congress in Brussels in February 1927 in order to expand and intensify the efforts of the Communists to win support among the colonial and dependent peoples of Africa and Asia.[20] Apart from supporters of national independence movements, the League was a conglomeration of pacifists, left Social Democrats, anarchists, syndicalists, non-party intellectuals, and Communists. At the founding congress of the League, a conference of the youth delegates was arranged. Representatives from various colonial lands, as well as from the French and British Young Communist Leagues, attended. The conference called upon the League to form associated youth bureaus and to propagate the aims of the League among young workers. The ECCYI called on the Communist youth organizations "to participate actively in the organization of youth sections of the League in different countries."[21]

Evidently these efforts did not meet with much early success, since two years later, just before the second congress of the League in July 1929, an international "anti-imperialist" youth conference was staged in Frankfurt, Germany.[22] The Communist Youth International, the Red Sports International, and other Communist organizations participated along with the various national delegations. This conference was used as a platform for propaganda on "imperialist preparations for war against the Soviet Union," and speakers depicted life for youth in the Soviet Union, the first "socialist" state, as being much better than in the "capitalist" countries. Though billed as politically "non-partisan," the meeting reflected the Comintern line almost completely.

Of special interest in the proceedings of this conference was the use of an International Preparatory Committee to make all the arrangements. This has become a favorite technique for maintaining a "non-partisan" façade for what is in fact a Communist event or activity.

The conference was sponsored openly, not by the CYI or any other Communist organization, but rather by a front in the form of an International Preparatory Committee. With Communists in control of the key posts, sympathetic non-Communists are added to the Committee in order to give the event an appearance of impartiality.

The Fifth Congress of the CYI in 1928 introduced what was called the "conveyor system"—the establishment of youth sections and youth commissions in the trade unions, in the military, and in cultural organizations.[23] Communist youth was to take a new tack to improve its effectiveness by penetrating existing youth groups, or forming new ones on a "non-party" basis.

The advent of Hitler to power in Germany created a radically new situation and threat to the international Communist movement but it was some time before it was realistically appraised by the Comintern. In March 1933 the ECCYI still proclaimed that "the main task of the [CYI] is to educate youth in the spirit of confidence in the Party, in the spirit of irreconcilable class hatred and struggle against fascist and bourgeois dictatorships which is concealed by democratic forms."[24] The Communist front organizations were busy organizing efforts to oppose fascism and the war that they saw threatening as a result of the Nazi rise to power, and the activities of the CYI soon became devoted almost exclusively to mobilizing youth of all countries in support of these front activities. Still castigating and refusing to cooperate with the Social Democratic organizations and their leaders, the ECCYI issued an appeal to all Socialist, Christian, trade union, Communist, and unorganized youth to set up anti-war committees in factories, schools, and wherever else youth was active.[25] An important result of these efforts was the convocation of the First World Youth Congress Against War in Paris in September 1933.

According to Communist sources, the Congress participants were divided into 553 "non-party," 3 Christians, 20 pacifists, 7 "secular Republicans," 111 young Socialists,

1 anarchist, 387 young Communists, and 10 others.[26] The manifesto issued by the Congress supported the Soviet Union, which it saw under threat of attack by the big "imperialist" powers (Britain, France, the United States). The Congress went on record against the Versailles Treaty, the League of Nations (a council of the "imperialist" victors), and "bourgeois democracy." The tasks that the Congress presumed to set for all youth who were against fascism and war included:

1. Making every place where workers gathered "a fortress of the struggle against fascism and war," and exposing the production and transportation of war materials.
2. Opposing all chauvinist and militarist activity in the mass sport and labor service (e.g., the New Deal-sponsored CCC) organizations.
3. Winning of support in the military forces, and among the young recruits.
4. Defending the young Communists and other young workers against fascist persecution.
5. Forming a network of committees embracing all universities and schools.
6. Preparation for the year 1934 of a series of national congresses of youth against fascism and war.[27]

By 1934 the Comintern had given up its revolutionary expectations and had recognized that concerted action with the Social Democrats and all "anti-fascists" was necessary in order to combat the Nazi menace. This turnabout in Comintern policy became known as the Popular Front, and was characterized by attempts to rally all forces of the left, center, and even the right against the threat of fascism. The new line took the form of overtures from the Communists to other organizations for cooperation and joint action. It also involved an intensification of front activities.

The shift in line to the Popular Front was transmitted to all Communist organizations at the Seventh Con-

gress of the Comintern in July-August 1935, and specifically to Communist youth at the Sixth CYI Congress that
followed in September-October. The main theme of the
youth congress was "unity of all non-fascist youth."[28] In
order to achieve this, the Communist youth organizations
were to change in character from small, sectarian groups
to "mass non-party organizations, including in their ranks
not only Communists, but also Socialists and non-party
youth—all the young people who are ready to fight
against fascism and reaction, for peace and freedom."[29]
The main target was the new Nazi dictatorship in Germany, with its persecution of the Communists and its
potential threat to the U.S.S.R.

The first step in the "struggle for unity" was to join
the Young Communist Leagues in each country with the
Young Socialist Leagues. In order to get around the opposition of the Socialist parties, the Young Communist Leagues
were to establish United Fronts with Socialist youth, form
unity committees for common action, and where possible
take direct steps to unify the two Leagues. The ultimate
objective was to be the formation of a single youth international.

Actual cooperation took different forms, and was
effected on different bases. In France the young Communists formed committees, councils, and associations in
which young Socialists and other youths participated for
some specific objective, usually economic, cultural, or
involving the political rights of youth. In England,
cooperation between young Communists and non-Communists was primarily on the issue of peace. In the United
States, the main arena of cooperation was the American
Youth Congress.

Communist youth in fascist countries (Germany, Italy,
and most of Eastern Europe) was to join with all other
"anti-fascist" youth and work inside fascist youth organizations. This involved support for the non-fascist youth
organizations that still existed in the fascist countries,
particularly Catholic youth organizations. Communist
youth was to avoid isolation, and therefore illegal work,

which was to be continued, would be subordinated to the legal and semi-legal mass work.

The Bulgarian Communist, Georgi Dimitrov, then head of the Comintern, criticized the Communist youth organizations at the Seventh Comintern Congress. Their fundamental weakness lay in their attempts to copy the Communist parties and their forms and methods of work. Where the Communist parties had to retain their independence, the Young Communist Leagues did not have as great a need to retain their separate identity. Speaking to the CYI congress that followed, he said that youth needed to find ways "to create a *new type* of mass organization of youth in the capitalist countries . . . ."[30] The first step in this direction was to change the character of the Young Communist Leagues from narrow circles of convinced adherents, concerned primarily with abstract politics, to large organizations concerned with educating young people. The next step would be to get the other youth organizations, especially the Socialist ones, to build a single mass organization of working youth, *outside the parties*.

Heretofore cultural organizations, clubs, groups and circles, political education courses, economic organizations (trade unions), and groups of unemployed youths, young peasants, young women, and students had been "subsidiary" or "auxiliary" organizational forms of Communist youth activity, acting only as "transmission belts" of Communist influence from the political, sectarian youth organization to the masses of young people. The Sixth CYI Congress changed this organizational concept. The Communist youth organization was now to expand so as to encompass all of these activities directly.

A drastic reorganization of the Communist Youth International was also called for by the Sixth Congress. Conditions for acceptance into the CYI were to be widened so that not only Communist organizations could join it, but also Socialist, "national emancipation," "national revolutionary," and "anti-fascist" youth organizations seeking international cooperation. The internal life of the CYI was to be reorganized in order to give the greatest amount of autonomy to affiliates.[31] Despite these provisions, there is no evidence to indicate that the CYI was able to attract any new, non-Communist organization to membership. There apparently was a growth in CYI membership during the late 1930s, but this only reflected a general growth in the Communist youth organizations as a reaction to the Nazi threat in Europe.

Within the youth movement, the efforts at forming a United Front with the Socialists were the most pronounced in the German, French, and Spanish Communist youth organizations. In late 1935 the illegal German Communist youth organization met in Brussels and called for unity with the still legal, but harried, Socialist youth in the struggle against Hitler.[32] The German Communists called specifically for an agreement on how Communist and Socialist youth could best work together within the *Hitler Jugend*, the state-controlled youth organization that monopolized all youth activities. They also called for the merger of the Socialists and the Communists into one unified youth organization.[33] However, as the Communists also continued to attack the Socialists under the guise of "genuine criticism," it is not surprising that the latter would have nothing to do with these proposals.

A further inhibiting factor was the continued adherence of the Socialist party leaders to the traditional Socialist view that youth should stay out of politics. If agreements were to be made, it would be between the Socialist and Communist parties. This opposition was overcome in France, however, when the Young Socialist League and the Young Communist League signed a national agreement for unity of action in March 1935.[34] But the Socialists still continued to oppose all Communist efforts to create a united youth organization.

In March 1936 the Executive Committees of the Young Socialist League and the Young Communist League in Spain voted to approve the report of a joint unity committee recommending that a single youth organization be formed.[35] In the midst of the Spanish Civil War, the Communists had succeeded in winning enough support within the Spanish Socialist youth movement, or at least within its leadership, to bring that organization to terms. The Socialist Youth International, however, did not approve this action and eventually, in the summer of 1939, expelled the united organization, which was by then under Communist influence.[36] Other "united" youth organizations that had been formed by a Socialist-Communist merger were also expelled at this time, including a group in Belgium, the British Labor League of Youth, and the International Federation of Socialist Students.[37]

The main activities of the CYI after 1934 consisted of organizing and supporting a large number of youth front organizations and demonstrations. A World Congress of Students Against War and Fascism was held in Brussels under CYI sponsorship at the end of December 1934 in order to develop a common platform for students in the "fight against war and fascism."[38] The educational systems and student life in the "capitalist" countries were attacked and criticized, while those in the Soviet Union were praised.

The congress of the International Federation of Socialist Students, held in Oxford, England, in July 1936, was the scene of vigorous action to win support for unification with Communist students, and the congress did finally decide, over the opposition of several delegations, to unite with the Communists.[39]

The most important activities of the CYI in this period, however, were the two World Youth Congresses that took place in 1936 in Geneva, Switzerland, and in 1938 at Vassar College in Poughkeepsie, New York. These gatherings of youth from many countries and from many different backgrounds were sponsored by the International Federation of League of Nations Societies for the purpose of discussing ways and means of maintaining peace and containing Nazi expansionism.

The preparations for the first congress were made by an Organizing Committee composed of representatives, adult and youth, from the various affiliated national League of Nations Societies. Later, representatives of

major international youth organizations were co-opted.
Still others were added after the agenda and the rules
had been established. It is not clear just when the Communist representatives first participated, but it is apparent
from the proceedings that non-Communists were definitely
in control of the meeting. German, Japanese, and Italian
youth representatives had been active in the preparations,
but when the Organizing Committee decided to invite the
Communists to join, these representatives left and did not
participate further. In addition, most of the Catholic
youth organizations decided not to participate with the
Communists.

The basic themes of the congress, around which the
discussions took place, were:

1. The organization of peace.
2. The problem of peaceful change—collective security
   and disarmament.
3. The economic and social organization of the world.
4. The moral, religious, philosophical, and other bases
   of peace (including the Communist point of view).[40]

The line followed by the Communist representatives
at the congress was that the youth of the Soviet Union
was ready to cooperate with all organizations, or their
representatives, whatever their political or religious affiliation, in defense of peace and against war. This followed
precisely the position of the Comintern at this time. The
leader of the Komsomol, speaking on the Communist point
of view, regretted that many Catholic representatives were
not present. In an uncharacteristic mood of reasonableness, the Russian speaker stated that while Communist
youth was atheistic, it opposed religious restrictions and
persecutions. This attitude was probed by delegates from
various religious organizations, who hoped that Christian
propaganda could be disseminated within the Soviet
Union. The Russian representatives assured the delegates
that such efforts would be welcomed. In fact, however,
there was never any effort by the Soviet authorities to

allow dissemination of religious propaganda inside the Soviet Union. A further appeal, however, was made to the religious delegates, as well as to the Christian organizations not represented, by the French Communist youth leader, Raymond Guyot. He set forth the terms on which the Communists believed Christian-Communist cooperation was possible:

1. Condemnation of war as a method of settling differences between peoples.
2. Respect for the independence of all peoples whether strong or weak and whatever the race to which they belong.
3. Common will to lift humanity out of slavery and poverty and to alleviate the material and moral lot of all men and particularly the young so that adolescents may grow up into strong human beings capable of the highest virtues and if need be of heroism.[41]

Who could disagree with these objectives? The difficulty, of course, was that while the Communists might say that they supported such principles, what they did in practice might be an entirely different matter. Yet at this time there were enough people, young and old, who so wanted to avoid war, and who so wanted to believe that they were active in support of measures to prevent a war, that they fell victim to these siren songs. Accordingly, the first World Youth Congress accepted Communist participation in its proceedings and affiliation with its objectives. The Congress came out strongly for collective security and a policy capable of making the League of Nations able to enforce its decisions. Its more general appeal was to the youth of the world to unite in defense of peace, and to launch a youth crusade for peace.

What did the Communists get out of this congress? In the first place, they had gained a wide international forum for their views. In the second place, they had taken a long step toward respectability by being accepted as participants. They could now point to the fact that they were part of the general fight against war and fascism and for peace, which, in turn, made it easier to further their own objectives.

After the first World Youth Congress, a series of national youth peace committees was established in over twenty-five countries. Cooperating were organizations of various political orientations, from the Socialist Youth International and the Communist Youth International to the YM-YWCA. Notably absent from these joint enterprises were the large Catholic youth organizations and important parts of the Socialist youth organizations in France, Denmark, and other countries. These peace committees collected food and money for Republican Spain; they demanded that their governments sell arms to the Republican forces. In England after 1938 the cry was for Chamberlain's resignation and the formation of a government that would "not capitulate to the fascist aggressors."[42] In the United States neutrality and isolationism were attacked, and the U.S. government was exhorted to collaborate with the democratic countries of Europe "for the defense of peace." This position was certainly a respectable one at the time, and those who supported it were by no means all Communists or Communist supporters. The Communist position simply coincided with a popu. point of view, a fact that the Communists utilized to their best advantage, as may well be seen from the history of an American youth organization.

THE AMERICAN YOUTH CONGRESS

A student of the activities of youth in the United States during the 1930s has written that "the major form in which the organized activity of youth found its expression was the American Youth Congress."[43] The AYC was founded in August 1934 at a meeting in New York, held under the auspices of New York University. The idea of an American Youth Congress had come from a young woman who wanted young people "to get together and discuss their problems, under the guidance of prominent older people."[44] At the founding congress, however, a Young Communist League-Young Socialist League-led group succeeded in gaining control of the movement. The meeting adopted resolutions opposing the Roosevelt administration, and demanding the abolition of the Civilian Conservation Corps (CCC) because "it is a step toward militarism and fascism."[45] The meeting also demanded that American youth carry on militant anti-war action, and created a committee to establish a permanent organization.

In the spring of 1935, Socialist and Communist youth was active in sponsoring a series of "strikes against war" on the campuses of many American universities. The purpose of these demonstrations was to involve students in political questions, and to gain an audience for Communist-Socialist views. In succeeding years similar "strikes" were organized, the leading force being the American Student Union, a student counterpart of AYC. The support of several Christian youth movements and sections of the National Student Federation of America gave these demonstrations the appearance of broader support. The demonstrations were in fact supported by many liberals, pacifists, and religious leaders.

With the initiation of the Popular Front, policy in the Comintern and national Communist organizations in 1934-35, the Communist leadership of the newly formed AYC turned to developing it into a mass non-party, anti-fascist youth organization.

The second American Youth Congress meeting in July 1935, however, was restricted almost exclusively to the young Communist and young Socialist movements. An example of the front tactic of the Communists in preparing mass meetings was seen during the preparations for this congress. The Young Peoples' Socialist League opposed Communist efforts to pack the National Council of the AYC, arguing that many representatives of autonomous, "nonpartisan" groups actually did not speak for anyone, and were placed on the Council only in order to give the Young Communist League an assured majority.[46] In 1935 at least fourteen of the forty National Council members were actually "open members of the Young Communist League, or consistent fellow-travellers."[47] The fourteen, however, represented an organized caucus that, through determined and disciplined action, could control the activities of the entire Council. Communist control of the smaller executive body, the National Administrative Council, which appointed all committees, issued all publicity, and represented the AYC in dealings with other organizations and government bodies, enabled the Communists to further extend their grip on the AYC.[48] Furthermore, by electing non-Communists to the National Council who were unlikely to appear often at meetings (due usually to the press of other business), the hard-core Communists could always control the necessary quorum.[49] This was an early example of how a Communist minority could, and can, capture and control an initially non-Communist organization, while maintaining a façade of unity and "non-partisanship."

The second meeting of the AYC supported the Soviet Union's "struggle for peace," but did not discuss in specific terms any of the issues it faced. A general statement entitled "The Declaration of Rights of American Youth" did not say what the AYC would do, but only put forth a program for "good" and against "evil." This lack of precision made it possible for the Communist leadership to carry out whatever policies it wished under a broad and widely accepted statement of vague principles. It also contributed to the erection of a façade of unity. A "bandwagon" psychology was also carefully nurtured to exploit the tendency of many youths to join where others were joining.

From 1936 through 1938 the Communists solidified their hold on the American Youth Congress by moving increasingly toward complete support of the New Deal's foreign and domestic programs, which enabled them to win support from large numbers of liberals and non-Communist youths, and also to follow the Comintern line. The AYC thus became a Popular Front, pro-New Deal alliance under artfully veiled Communist control.[50]

The third session of the AYC, in 1936, saw the young Socialists split with the Communists. The former wanted to reduce Communist control over the organization by limiting the powers of paid functionaries, and by drafting a specific action program.[51] After their defeat on these issues, the Socialists ceased to participate in the AYC other than nominally, turning instead to building their own organization. Yet during 1937 the AYC was able to develop close links with various New Deal agencies, such as the National Advisory Committee of the National Youth Administration, a governmental agency.

The most active work of the AYC centered on the campaign for the American Youth Act, which had been drawn up by the National Council of the AYC in 1935. This draft act provided for a number of government-sponsored welfare activities on behalf of youth and students, yet, while no more radical than other welfare legislation of this period, it never got past committee hearings. Nevertheless in February 1937 the AYC mobilized 4000 young people to lobby for the act, and a delegation met with President Roosevelt and Mrs. Roosevelt.

At the fourth AYC meeting in 1937 a program fully supporting collective security was approved, appealing as it did not only to the Communists and their sympathizers but to all honest non-Communists who saw collective security as the best means of avoiding war and containing aggression.[52]

A high point in AYC activities was the second World Youth Congress in the summer of 1938. The American World Youth Congress Committee, which prepared for this meeting, was essentially a committee of the AYC.[53] It was chaired by the Executive Secretary of the AYC, and included representatives from many non-Communist organizations, such as the League of Nations Association, National Recreation Association, American Jewish Congress, International Student Seminar, National Student Federation of America, American Youth Hostel Association, New York State Federation of Churches, YWCA, Girl Scouts, YMCA, and the Foreign Policy Association.[54] The

Socialist Youth International and international Catholic and trade union groups only sent observers. The U.S. delegation was securely in the hands of the Young Communist League, while Socialists, pacifists, and isolationists were in a clear minority.[55]

The major outcome of the congress was a "Peace Pact," which committed the signatories to:

1. Promote international unity and fraternity among the youth.
2. Condemn aggression and the infringement of the independence of nations.
3. Win youth to an active struggle against aggression and war.
4. Press governments to assist victims of aggression and to apply sanctions against aggressors.
5. Condemn the bombardment of civilian populations.
6. Advocate the use of international machinery for settling disputes between nations.[56]

Except for the pacifists and isolationists, and those Marxists who condemned all attempts to support "imperialist" regimes, the "Peace Pact" appealed to a wide audience of young people. It supported the League of Nations, the "quarantining" of aggressors, and mutual assistance pacts.[57]

The Roosevelt administration supported the World Youth Congress. Indeed Mrs. Roosevelt had become a patron and supporter of the AYC, which supported the policies of the New Deal almost without reservation.[58] This honeymoon ended abruptly after the Nazi-Soviet Pact was signed in August 1939. The American Youth Congress' Communist leadership was forced to do a complete about-face. Nothing more was heard about collective security and support for the Roosevelt administration. The Popular Front and the unity of "anti-fascist" youth were suddenly obsolete. Old enemies became new friends, and old friends new enemies. Roosevelt was attacked for initiating the Lend-Lease program and increasing U.S. military expenditures. "The Yanks Are *Not* Coming" committees formed at this time received Communist support, as did isolationist and pacifist movements. The American Youth Congress came out against U.S. involvement in an "imperialist" war and was promptly deserted by many of its former followers. The hand of the Communists in the AYC was revealed even more forcefully on the heels of the Soviet invasion of Finland and the Winter War in 1939-1940. They argued now for anti-war unity, but they were not willing to condemn Soviet aggression, or to cooperate with groups that did so.

In France, the new Comintern line resulted in an immediate break between Communist and Socialist youth, and an abrupt end to the Popular Front. Communists did not reject the concept of national defense, but held that the best way to defend the "important" things in a nation (the rights of workers against the bourgeoisie) was to keep out of an "imperialist" war.

After the attack on the Soviet Union by Nazi Germany in June 1941, the Communist line underwent another abrupt reversal. Once again everything was to be done to defeat Hitler. The slogans under which Communist youth in the United States organized the annual International Youth Day in September 1941 included:

> Full, unlimited aid to Great Britain, the Soviet
>   Union, and all nations fighting for the military
>   defeat of German fascism!
> Defend America by defeating Hitler!
> For complete American partnership in the British-
>   Soviet alliance to destroy Hitler![59]

The Communist rationalization of these abrupt switches in line provides an interesting example of dialectical casuistry. Until June 1941, said the Communists, the war had been a two-sided "imperialist" war in which neither side fought for justice, but only for empire. However, the character of the war had been transformed by the attack on the Soviet Union. Now it was a "just" war against fascism. Imperialism and justice had been present all along, said the Communist apologists—the former dominated prior to June 1941, the latter afterwards.

This new line brought a return to the United Front strategy and full collaboration with all "bourgeois" youth groups that supported the struggle against Hitler. Communist youth supported the USO, cooperated with all war relief societies and refugee aid committees, and participated in various community campaigns.

Finally, after the attack on the U. S. at Pearl Harbor in December 1941, the Communists adopted an air of patriotic fervor. The Young Communist League publication, *Clarity*, said in 1942 that "our Young Communist League is a loyal, patriotic organization of youth dedicated to serving our country in its war against fascist barbarism."[60] A local section of the Young Communist League in San Francisco formed itself into a Colin Kelly Club, after the U. S. Army Air Force pilot who became the first Congressional Medal of Honor winner.[61] All young Communists were exhorted to take the lead in "win-the-war" activities.[62]

The role of Communist youth as an instrument of Soviet policy was not forgotten, however. During 1943, the young Communists followed the Soviet government lead and propagandized for a "second front now." Recognizing that new methods for the continuation of its work were in order, the Young Communist League dissolved itself in October 1943 at a meeting in New York.[63] It decided to form a new and broader group that would include non-Communist youth. On the following day, American Youth for Democracy was formed, with leaders of the dissolved Young Communist League as permanent officers. AYD was described as "a mass, advanced anti-fascist youth organization in which the Communists play the leading role."[64]

During the war Communist youth throughout the world was preoccupied almost exclusively with the defense of the Soviet Union and the defeat of Nazi Germany. Yet the future was not neglected; even during the war, the ground was being laid for the extension of Communist influence after the end of hostilities.

3/Chapter
The International Communist Youth and Student Movements in the Post-War Period (1945 — 1953)

The switch by all Communist organizations in the mid-1930s to the tactics of the Popular Front signified a basic change within the Communist movement. Earlier, promotion of Communist ideology and support of Soviet foreign policy had existed side by side as the primary concerns of Communist parties and the Communist youth organizations. From the mid-1930s, however, the ultimate goal of a Communist society was increasingly subordinated to the contemporary requirements of the Soviet state. A result of this change in orientation was that the obviously partisan character of Communist organizations came more and more to be hidden behind a façade of "non-partisan," "representative" unity with many other political and social groups. The immediate objectives and propaganda slogans of the Communist movement no longer stressed the overthrow of the "capitalist-imperialist exploiters" and establishment of the dictatorship of the proletariat. The emphasis was now on "peaceful coexistence" and harmony of all "anti-fascist" political forces. This new line was an important reason for the dissolution of the Comintern and the Communist Youth International in 1943, as the Soviet Union sought to fortify the image of "unity" with its Western allies.

During and after World War II the Communists consistently tried to profit from their experience in the twenties and thirties. Having had by far their greatest successes when they had used United and Popular "front" techniques, rather than clearly partisan organizations, Communist wartime and post-war activities were accordingly directed toward creating new and more widely based international "front" organizations. Among the many that emerged after World War II were the World Federation of Democratic Youth (WFDY) and the International Union of Students (IUS).

WORLD FEDERATION OF DEMOCRATIC YOUTH

The international efforts of the Communists to organize the youth of the world on this new basis began almost as soon as the Soviet Union was in the war. Young Communists throughout the world immediately became active in the efforts to mobilize youth against Hitler and in support of the Soviet Union.[1] Their activities were centered in London, where in November 1941 a meeting was held of youth representatives from many nationalities and of many political colorations. The committee that arranged this meeting constituted itself as an International Youth Council, and decided to hold an international youth conference in London in the fall of 1942. The Komsomol sent a delegation, which seems to have spent most of its time urging a second front in the West rather than discussing youth problems. The conference was more concerned, however, with discussing the actions to be taken in the post-war period to improve the lot of young people. To this end it established a World Youth Council (WYC), located in London, whose purposes were: "(1) to inspire youth to victory, thus bringing closer the day when youth could live happier, freer lives, and (2) to link the youth organizations of the world together."[2]

In July 1943 a Western Hemisphere Youth for Victory Conference was held in Mexico City. Participants from fourteen Latin American countries, the United States, and Canada voted to cooperate with the World Youth Council.

The November 1942 London conference had also created an Executive Committee for the WYC, and with the end of the war in Europe, this body prepared another international youth conference in London for the fall of 1945. The purpose of this conference was to found a new international youth organization.

Meeting in Albert Hall in a mood of genuine enthusiasm, the conference was opened by messages of greeting from President Truman and Prime Minister Attlee.[3] The atmosphere in which the conference met can perhaps best be understood by quoting from the report of the U. S delegation:

> Regardless of the conduct of the meetings *per se*, regardless of the decisions reached, regardless of the differences in approach and background, there was a fundamental and powerful feeling of understanding and cooperation for effective guarantees that there shall be a stable and lasting peace, and the opportunity for a happy life for all future generations.[4]

The conference and its discussions were organized into three main sections: (1) "Youth Fights for Freedom and a Better World"; (2) "The Post-War Needs of the Youth"; and (3) "The Organization of International Youth Cooperation." Above all there was a pervasive desire to preserve unity. The resolutions were phrased in general, idealistic terms so that all delegates could support them. This resulted in the absence of any mention of Communism. The resolutions proposed by the U. S. delegation on international security and the self-determination of peoples are a good example. They ignored the problems within Soviet-occupied areas, and stressed that continued cooperation between the U. S., the U.S.S.R., Britain, China, and France would be essential for world peace. Despite its non-

Communist composition, the political orientation of the U. S. delegation showed through in its draft resolution on self-determination of peoples, where it was stated that "American imperialist domination of the countries of Latin and South America should be ended . . . ."[5]

The conference approved and adopted a constitution for a new international youth organization, to be called the World Federation of Democratic Youth.[6] The WFDY was to be governed by a Congress composed of representatives from each of its member organizations, to meet every three years. To supervise the work of an Executive Committee and Secretariat, a Council was to meet once a year. The Congress was to elect the Executive Committee to run day-to-day affairs. The headquarters of the WFDY were established in Paris.

Communists were represented openly by only about 3 per cent of the delegates. But there were large numbers of delegates unidentifiable by political orientation who spoke for national youth councils, "coordinating committees," cultural and educational organizations, students, and trade unionists. Within each national delegation there was a Communist fraction, often unidentifiable as such, which usually exerted more influence than its numbers would suggest. The majority of the delegates to the conference, however, seem to have been non-Communist.

INTERNATIONAL UNION OF STUDENTS

In March 1945 the British National Union of Students convened a meeting of students from various Allied nations in order to plan for an international student federation.[7] As between Communists and non-Communists, this meeting "agreed to disagree" on political issues and decided to plan an international student conference for London in November.

After the end of the war in Europe, however, students in Czechoslovakia also evolved plans to hold an international students meeting in Prague. In August representatives from both the London and the Prague groups agreed that both meetings should take place, but that neither was to be an official international student conference.

The London meeting took place as scheduled in November 1945, shortly after the youth conference at which the WFDY was founded. The majority at this students' meeting was also non-Communist, and one of the big issues that were debated was whether or not to affiliate with the new youth organization. The Soviet representatives at the youth conference had opposed the formation of a separate student organization. They wanted the students to be a section of the WFDY, very much as they have always been incorporated in the Komsomol. When the representatives from the West insisted, however, the Russians gave way and accepted the formation of two organizations. At the students' conference, the Communists thus naturally favored a close tie between the planned international student organization and the WFDY. A final decision on this issue, as well as on the founding of the student international, was postponed until the summer of 1946, when a constitutional convention could be held.

After the London conference of November 1945, some of the participants went to Prague and joined in the discussions at the second meeting that was in progress there. Contrary to the understanding reached in August, the Czechoslovak Communists were attempting to turn this meeting into a "founding congress" and to establish a Communist-controlled international student organization. But this apparent aberration came to nothing, since the pre-war Communist organizational form had been discarded in favor of behind-the-scenes control of organizations that could claim wider support.

The London student conference had elected an International Preparatory Committee to plan for the constitutional convention. The seat of the IPC, as well as the location of the convention, was to be in Paris, likewise the new home of the WFDY. Despite the fact that the Communists had been in a minority at the conference that created it, the IPC turned out to be dominated by Communists, or those under strong Communist influence. The broad mandate given to the IPC—"to take any action in the interests of the students"—[8] thus gave them free rein to arrange the international student conference to suit their own purposes.

First, wide powers were given to a small, Communist-controlled executive body of the IPC. Then a majority of the IPC supported the proposal of the Russian delegate to move the seat of the IPC, and the location of the constitutional convention, from Paris to Prague because the Czechoslovak National Union of Students, like the Czechoslovak government, had come under the control of a Socialist-Communist coalition. The Communists within the student organization had captured control of its international activities, and hence the Secretariat that was formed in Prague to assist the IPC in its work was composed almost exclusively of young Czechoslovak Communists. The coloration that the IPC had assumed was evident from anti-Western, pro-Soviet statements that it issued on several controversial political questions, and from the fact that permanent representatives were sent by the IPC to other Communist-front organizations then being formed—the WFDY, the World Federation of Trade Unions (WFTU), and the Women's International Democratic Federation (WIDF).

Finally the planned international student conference did meet in Prague in August 1946 and founded the International Union of Students (IUS). The majority of the delegates were *not* Communists, but the Communists were nevertheless able to win general approval for their positions, and to win eleven of the sixteen seats on the Executive Committee of the new organization.

Discussions over the IUS constitution revealed the differences between the Communists and non-Communists in full. After much debate, the Communist proposal to establish the permanent headquarters of the IUS in Prague was approved. With the administrative apparatus thus continuing under the control of the Czechoslovak Communists, full assertion by the Communists of control over the IUS would only be a matter of time. However, the Communists lost on making the Executive Committee—which would conduct the day-to-day business of the IUS—a policy-making body. Instead, this function fell to a Congress that was to meet every three years, and an annual Council. In practice, however, the Executive Committee still became the most important body in the IUS.

When the minority accepted the fact that some tie to the WFDY was inevitable, it fought successfully against membership in the WFDY and for an autonomous association with it. The tie was to be even looser by putting the provision for association in the by-laws, where a simple majority vote was sufficient to disaffiliate. The Communists, however, insisted that the IUS become a tightly centralized organization and won retention of a clause in the Constitution that required member organizations to carry out all decisions of the governing bodies of the IUS, and to support organizations with aims similar to those of the IUS. Finally, the composition of the Executive Committee was dictated in advance by the Russians, who decided who and from what country would hold what office.

How were the Communists, in a minority at the conferences that created both the WFDY and the IUS, able to win control of these organizations? In order to understand the reasons one must reconstruct the conditions and mood of those early post-war days.

One result of the Second World War was that it created as never before a deep desire for peace and a better world. The early post-war years were permeated by an aura of intense idealism. And while this atmosphere existed throughout the world, it was most pronounced in Europe. It was here that not only the war, but the terror of the fascist and Nazi dictatorships, had been most keenly felt. Many people were emotionally so strongly tied to efforts to prevent a recurrence of the past that they could not, or would not, see the realities that were unfolding before them. It was in this favorable climate that the Communists took steps to institutionalize the wartime cooperation against fascism. For an outgrowth of this idealism was the belief that it was essential to preserve wartime unity, and that cooperation between Russia and the West was essential in order to prevent a recurrence of the past.

The fact that many of the delegates, Communist and non-Communist, to the international youth and student conferences had been in the resistance was an important factor in enabling the Communist-influenced leadership of these conferences to win support by playing on emotions. The Communists were able to stir up the delegates and create an atmosphere in which all opposition, and all moves to limit the power of the Communist leadership, could be attacked as "fascist." "Progress" and "democracy" were skillfully associated with Communist proposals. Any action that might disrupt "unity" thus could be made to come under attack, and this, in turn, proved a powerful brake on full and free discussion.

The general turn to the left in European politics after the war also contributed to the creation of an atmosphere favorable to the Communists. The Labor Party was voted into office in Great Britain in the early summer of 1945. Communists participated in the coalition governments formed in France, Italy, Belgium, Czechoslovakia, and Austria, and made strong electoral showings in most of these countries. Furthermore, the cooperation with the Communists that had become respectable during the war continued to be so in the immediate post-war period.

Also of vital importance to the assertion of Communist control over what at first were basically non-Communist movements was the discipline of the Communist groups. All Communists adhered to the same line, and supported the same proposals, while the non-Communists were divided into various groups supporting various proposals. Minority Communist factions within national delegations, through disciplined action, were usually able to dominate their delegations, and they were also able to control international conferences by voting as a bloc and appealing to non-Communists with pleas for unity.

Finally, by taking the initiative in the organizing efforts in 1945, the Communists were able to control the preparations for the post-war international youth and student conferences. The program and procedures, while following democratic patterns, were arranged so that the results of the conferences served the interests of the Communists. They could control the seating of delegates.[9] They dominated the credentials committee at the Prague Congress in August 1946. Few if any non-Communist student organizations were represented that were clearly anti-Communist. In part this was due to the unwillingness of the latter to participate, which in turn gave the Communists the chance to pick and choose, making sure that any non-Communist majority would be a pliable one. Difficulties arose at Prague over the credentials of a number of delegations, particularly those from India, Italy, and Spain. In the outcome either small Communist minority groups, or clearly unrepresentative Communist-influenced organizations, were seated, in preference to the larger, representative but non-Communist student organizations in the countries concerned.

THE ROAD INTO ISOLATION

The WFDY created in London in November 1945 adopted a clearly pro-Soviet attitude from the beginning. Although it contained a number of non-Communist youth organizations, they had almost no influence. In contrast to the IUS, the minority that wanted the WFDY to be a genuinely representative and non-partisan organization was too small to have any serious impact on its policies. Apparently having given up hope of winning significant support from non-Communist youth organizations, there was less need for the Communists to compromise with the non-Communists who did belong. Moreover, many youth organizations were not interested in joining the WFDY because groups such as the Boy Scouts, Boys Clubs, and religious and party-affiliated youth groups (Socialist, Christian Democrat, etc.) usually had constitutions prohibiting them from engaging in explicitly partisan political activity. Thus while the WFDY continued to present itself as a "representative" youth international, most of its membership outside the Communist countries was made up of small front organizations or individual groups that were members of larger representative youth organizations in their respective countries.

The WFDY began its activities at the first meeting of its Council in Paris in July 1946.[10] Plans were laid for a World Youth Festival, the first of a series of intensive propaganda demonstrations. The Council decided to dispatch a delegation to Germany "to study the situation of youth" in the defeated country, which was more likely in fact intended to organize support for the then developing Communist youth organization, *Freie Deutsche Jugend* (Free German Youth). Denied entry to the Western zones, this delegation had nothing but praise for the situation in the Soviet zone of occupation, and for the FDJ.

In September 1946, the WFDY began the publication in several languages of its monthly magazine, *World Youth*.

The World Youth Festival held in Prague in the summer of 1947 was the first in a series of biannual gatherings organized jointly by the WFDY and the IUS.[11] The glorification of Stalin and the life of Soviet youth and students, and the depiction of life in the U. S. in terms of gross distortion of factual situations (lynchings, racial disorders, economic inequities), characterized the approach of its sponsors. What happened was a faithful reflection of the radical change in Soviet foreign policy in process at this time. Participation in coalition governments in Western Europe was being abandoned, the Iron Curtain was descending, and the world was being divided into two hostile "imperialist" and "peace-loving" camps.[12]

The subordination of the WFDY to the Soviet cold-war propaganda machine was made clear when the second session of the Council met in Prague immediately after the Festival and condemned the U. S. for imperialism—in Europe and all over the globe.[13] This second WFDY Council meeting also confirmed the political nature of the organization when it rejected a British and Scandinavian resolution that would have limited the WFDY to primarily cultural affairs. It was not only the political character of the WFDY but its partisan outlook that was expressed here. The Western powers were attacked as reactionary and fascist, and the Soviet occupation of Eastern Europe praised.

Of more interest than the WFDY are developments within the IUS. Not only were the students and their organizations more politically active, and a more influential political factor, but an active non-Communist minority in the IUS continued for some time in hopes of bringing about changes in the policies of the Communist leadership.

Representatives of the various national student organizations had formed an international organization at Prague, but then they had to return home to have their actions ratified by their respective organizations. In the case of the U. S. this meant the formation of a national student organization, as none had existed before. While this process was under way, the Communists were consolidating their control over the IUS. In February 1947 a Secretariat was formed as an official body (to consist of the President, General Secretary, and the other Executive Committee members who lived in Prague "or held key posts"), to be responsible "in the absence of the Executive for the development of all policies."[14]

The Communist-non-Communist differences in the Executive Committee and the Secretariat appeared early. In 1947 the IUS turned its attention to Asia and sent its Yugoslav Vice-President—Tomovic—along with a WFDY organizing team to visit several Asian countries. At the same time the liberal-democratic International Student Service, primarily a non-political service and relief organization with headquarters in Geneva, planned a conference in Asia to discuss what could and should be done to aid students in that area. The Communist President and General Secretary of the IUS—Joseph Grohman of Czechoslovakia and Tom Madden of the United Kingdom —sought to have Tomovic instructed to discourage Asian participation in the ISS conference because "fascists were infiltrating it [ISS]," but the American Vice-President, William Ellis, refused to agree or to support efforts to have a rival WFDY - IUS conference. Matters came to a head at the May 1947 session of the Executive Committee, where the Russian and American Vice-Presidents clashed. Despite the opposition of Ellis, the Communist leadership was able to get its way, but because of it they were forced to go behind his back. Eventually the joint WFDY - IUS conference took place in Calcutta in early 1948, but was concerned more with political questions and clarifying the then current Communist line for Asian Communist youth than with specific youth problems.

Another point of conflict was the matter of elections. The Constitution called for annual elections by the Council. In the discussion of the agenda for the annual Council meeting, the Communists attempted to dispose of this electoral "bother" by proposing that since the present Executive Committee was doing such a good job, there was no need for an election. After long, heated, and persistent argument, Ellis did make his point, but it was in a losing cause, since the elections returned the same Communist-dominated leadership, with Ellis and one or two other non-Communists left to struggle in the minority.

The first annual meeting of the IUS Council took place in Paris in August 1947 at a time of increasing political tension.[15] The civil war was raging in Greece, and the Truman Doctrine (by which the U.S. extended assistance to the Greek and Turkish governments) had been announced in March. In early May the French Communists had been expelled from the Cabinet. U.S. Secretary of State George Marshall had made his famous speech at Harvard University in June launching the Marshall Plan. In the same month, a Foreign Ministers Conference in Paris discussing that plan broke up in deadlock. The Communists soon began denouncing the Marshall proposals as evidence of U.S. "imperialism," and shortly after the IUS Council session the Soviet, East European, French, and

Italian Communist parties joined to form the Communist Information Bureau (Cominform). The declaration of the conference founding the Cominform ended wartime "unity" with the "capitalist" countries by enunciating the doctrine of "the two camps." The world was thus divided into "imperialist" and "peace-loving" camps, the former headed by the U. S., and the latter by the Soviet Union. These two camps were said to be in total conflict, and the latter bound to be victorious.

The IUS Council session made even clearer the increasingly partisan association of the IUS, yet most of the non-Communist delegates returned home still supporting the continuation of membership by their organizations —but with safeguards. The desire for unity within the non-Communist student organizations remained strong and led to repeated efforts to work out solutions of differences, thus avoiding a break.[16] Many non-Communists also looked upon the IUS as an open door in the Iron Curtain—a door through which Western democratic ideas could be spread among students who received no objective information.

While the IUS was falling further under Communist control, the students in the U. S. were taking steps to form a representative national student organization.[17] This National Student Association was formed in the summer of 1947 at a conference in Madison, Wisconsin. After hearing representatives from the U. S. delegation to the Prague Congress (August 1946), the conference decided to have the new NSA affiliate with the IUS, but only under the following conditions: (1) the NSA was to be the sole representative of the IUS in the United States; (2) the NSA was to have the freedom to accept or reject IUS decisions; (3) a minority report was to be appended to all published IUS decisions; (4) the IUS was to be in no way involved with the WFDY; and (5) procedures for disaffiliating from the IUS were to be made easy. If accepted by the IUS, it is clear that these stipulations would have changed that organization from a tightly centralized Communist body into a Communist-run propaganda forum in

which non-Communists would have full freedom of discussion. A negotiating team from the NSA was to go to
Prague in the summer of 1948, and meanwhile the U. S.
would continue to participate in the IUS. William Ellis
was confirmed in his position as American Vice-President
of the IUS by the founding conference of the National
Student Association.

Events, however, were to overtake these plans. In
February 1948 the Communists staged a coup in
Czechoslovakia and took over the government and with
it the Czechoslovak national student organization. All
power was assumed by "action committees," and right-
wing students were purged. In the aftermath of the coup,
a mass parade of non-Communist students demanding the
maintenance of parliamentary government was held in
Prague before the Presidential Palace. The Communist-
controlled police arrested the student leaders. When the
IUS Secretariat refused the demand by William Ellis for
a vigorous IUS protest against the takeover of the
Czechoslovak student organization and the arrest of the
student leaders, the temporary U. S. representative on the
Executive Committee resigned and Ellis recommended to
the NSA that it disaffiliate, even though it had not as yet
formally joined. The President of the NSA issued a statement terminating any relationship that had existed between the IUS and the NSA. Ellis then formally resigned
as the American IUS Vice-President.[18]

As a result of the Czech coup, the Danish student
organization suspended its membership, the Swedes disaffiliated, and the Swiss decided not to join.[19] The British
National Union of Students, whose representative on the
Executive Committee was a Communist and the General
Secretary of the IUS, decided after debate to remain a
member, but to play an active role in opposition.[20] The
British remained members until 1952. Then they left, but
returned again in 1954 on the basis of "associate membership," only to leave again after the events in Hungary
in 1956.

From 1948 until the death of Stalin in 1953, the

WFDY and the IUS followed almost slavishly the violent and virulent Soviet anti-Western propaganda campaigns. All meetings of these organizations were turned into demonstrations against the West, the "capitalist exploiters," and the "imperialists." All publications contained the crudest, grossest, and most distorted attacks on the non-Communist world. If the world was not in fact divided into two antagonistic and hostile camps by 1947, Communist propaganda from that time on had the result of creating so much mutual hostility as really to lead to such a division.

With its headquarters in Communist-controlled Prague, the IUS had the full support of its host government. The WFDY and other front organizations (WFTU, WIDF) were, however, based in Paris. There the Communists had more difficulties. The anti-Western propaganda of the front organizations in connection with the Korean war presently led the French government (in January 1951) to expel them, whereupon they all settled in Vienna, still a divided city in a divided country.[21]

Both the WFDY and the IUS quickly took steps after their founding to expand their membership and influence. The WFDY in early 1946, and again in early 1947, sent representatives to Greece to help in the formation of a youth organization along Communist lines.[22] A conference of the WFDY in Mexico City in April-May 1948 was organized to rally support in Latin America for the WFDY, and for the pro-Soviet policies it was following. In August 1948 the WFDY staged an International Conference of Working Youth in Warsaw as a protest demonstration against the Marshall Plan at which the U. S. was accused of imperialist designs on the Western European countries.

The most significant action of the WFDY and the IUS at this time, however, was the "Conference of Youth and Students of South East Asia Fighting for Freedom and Independence," held in Calcutta, India, in February 1948.[23] It has indeed been suggested that this conference was the occasion on which orders from Moscow were passed on to the Communist parties in Burma, Malaya, and Indonesia, where Communist insurrections broke out against the national governments in March, June, and September.[24] A more thorough study of this issue, however, has concluded that the role of the WFDY and the IUS was somewhat different, if no less important.

The Calcutta Conference was to have been held in Indonesia as a demonstration of sympathy for the Southeast Asian nationalists fighting for independence against the colonial powers—the Dutch in Indonesia, the French in Indo-China, and the British in Malaya. However, the WFDY Council meeting in Prague in August 1947 decided that in view of the Dutch-Indonesian conflict it would be better to postpone it until early 1948, and move it to Calcutta. More important, the Council was probably aware of the general change in policy adopted by the Soviet Union in the summer of 1947. The shift away from attempts to win power in the non-Communist countries through parliamentary means, and the acceptance of the division of the world into two camps, was naturally also reflected in the Asian policy of the Soviet Union. It now became a case of if you are not for us, you must be against us. Until this time the U.S.S.R. had followed a policy of cooperation with the major nationalist parties in Asia and of moderation of Communist opposition to the colonial powers. With the institution of the "two-camp" doctrine, however, those Asian nationalist governments and parties that were not overtly pro-Soviet were abruptly assumed to be against the U.S.S.R. and thus in the camp of the "imperialist" colonial powers.

The Calcutta Conference was effectively controlled by the IUS and WFDY representatives. The International Preparatory Committee that arranged the meeting had been Communist-dominated, and thus it controlled the agenda and the seating of the delegates. While many of the organizations represented were Communist-oriented, a considerable number were not overly sympathetic. The expression of the new Communist "two-camp" line quickly alienated these groups, with the result that a number of delegations left the meeting. The conference was continued, however, and took a position closely echoing the accentuated "United Front from below" view of the 1928-1935 period. The purpose was to bring the anti-colonial youth movements in Southeast Asia under WFDY and IUS control by winning the rank and file over to Communist views.

Within the IUS, meanwhile, attempts were being made to salvage something from the wreckage caused by the reaction of the non-Communist student organizations to the Czechoslovak coup. At the annual Council meeting in Paris in the summer of 1948 the attacks on the West were stepped up.[25] The Council supported the action of the Secretariat in February in refusing to protest the arrest of non-Communist Czech students. The disaffiliations that took place after the events in Czechoslovakia were condemned as reactionary moves that worked against student unity. The old magic of "unity" was losing its influence, however. William Ellis, having clearly spelled out the nature of the IUS for all to see in his letter of resignation, was singled out by the Council session for particularly harsh attack.

Despite these moves, however, the opposition within the IUS was not completely dead. The British National Union of Students and several other Western student organizations remained members, attempting to exercise a non-Communist influence from within the organization. At the 1948 Council meeting three factions were still in evidence—the Russian delegation controlled the delegates from the Communist-bloc countries; the Indian delegation, made up of Communists, controlled the delegates from the colonial countries; and the British delegation was the center of a much smaller, less united non-Communist bloc.[26] The main weapon in the hands of the minority Western bloc was the continuing desire of the Communists to present a picture of total unity. This enabled the minority to threaten to vote against the Main Resolution, which the Communists wanted passed unanimously. The means by which the Communists were able to achieve this unity is enlightening. A compromise resolution on the action of the Secretariat at the time of the Czech coup was approved unanimously, the pertinent section of it being worded as follows:

> Although we acknowledge that *some* Council members held the opinion that the actions of the Executive Secretariat in connection with the recent events in Czechoslovakia were incorrect and not impartial and would like to protest against this, *the majority* of the Council considers that the actions of the Executive Secretariat were correct . . . .[27]

By achieving a unanimous vote for this wording, the Communists were able to take the sting out of the non-Communist opposition, and even to make it appear that despite the minority view there was unanimous support for the majority opinion. This technique was used again to get unanimous approval of the Main Resolution. The effect of this was to put the non-Communist minority in the position of seemingly approving the partisan policies of the IUS.

"Unity" continued to be the principal demand, but the definition of "unity" remained that of a Communist monopoly over the student movement through the IUS. The IUS leadership was willing to make some minor concessions, but there was not the slightest indication of a basic change in policy. At the Council meeting in Sofia in the summer of 1949 the British and others refused to support the blatant distortions of events and conditions in the Western countries, or to support the causes pushed by the Communists. In order again to avoid an outright break, the Communists toned down their attacks and proposed a "compromise" Main Resolution. This included a sentence to the effect that "active preparations for war and indirect incitement to war have markedly increased *in certain countries*,"[28] leaving the reader of the resolution free to interpret for himself just which ones they were. Further on in the resolution, however, a speech of an American Senator was cited as a "glaring example of this action."[29]

The incident that finally brought the non-Communist minority to leave the IUS was the expulsion of the Yugoslav student organization. Nothing, indeed, could have furnished clearer proof of the extent to which the IUS had become a pliable tool of the Communists and of the Soviet Union in particular. Though obviously unrelated to student and youth affairs, a break had occurred in the summer of 1948 between the Soviet Union and Yugoslavia. Essentially at issue was the latter's national sovereignty and Marshal Tito's refusal to acknowledge Stalin's right to intervene in Yugoslavia's internal affairs. Forthwith, the headquarters of the Cominform were moved from Belgrade to Bucharest and a political and economic boycott was imposed on Yugoslavia by all other Communist countries and parties, a move that was promptly parroted by the IUS leadership.

At the time of the IUS Council meeting in Sofia the Yugoslavs were still members of the IUS, and one of the Vice-Presidents was a Yugoslav.[30] Yet when five Yugoslavs showed up for the meeting they were immediately arrested and later expelled from the country. The Western delegates took the matter up with Grohman, the Czech IUS President, but nothing was done. Although the Western delegates were not necessarily in full agreement with the Yugoslavs, they were attempting to maintain democratic procedures, and to avoid involving the organization in partisan Communist disputes. The issue was thus raised in the Presidium of the Council meeting, in the Steering Committee, and again on the floor, but all to no avail—the IUS leadership had no intention of taking a stand in opposition to that of the Soviet Communist Party.

The Executive Committee meeting in London in February 1950 became in effect a trial, or rather a "kangaroo court," of the Yugoslav student organization.[31] The majority attacked the Yugoslavs for, among other things, the persecution of "democratic" (i.e., pro-Stalinist) students. The tenor of the discussion that took place during the questioning of the Yugoslav representative can be seen from the following excerpt:

> *Berlinguer* [Italy, Communist]: Is it true that there are 4000 students in jail in Yugoslavia?
>
> *Bucevic* [Yugoslav representative]: This is a fiction.
>
> *Grohman* [IUS President]: So I understand that you refuse to reply?
>
> *Jenkins* [British NUS representative]: Bucevic has replied, and has said that the statement is a fiction.
>
> *Ascarate* [Spain, Communist]: On a point of order; we understand that the Yugoslav is being questioned, and it is very difficult if Jenkins interrupts with questions and answers.[32]

The Yugoslav "crimes" actually consisted of defending themselves in public against the Cominform charges, and of arranging an international conference outside the framework of the IUS, thus seeking "to split the unity of the international student movement." With only the British in opposition, the Executive Committee voted to expel the Yugoslavs from the IUS whereupon the British NUS decided to suspend its own membership until the next Council meeting. The British argued that they had done the same things as the Yugoslavs, but had not been attacked so violently, or expelled, but then neither had they offended Stalin and the Soviet Communist Party. Later, when the Council met in Prague, just before the Second IUS Congress in August 1950, the Executive Committee decision to expel the Yugoslavs was ratified, in violation of the Constitution, which provided that member organizations had the right to be present when their affairs were being discussed.

As had become the practice with congresses of Communist front organizations, this IUS Congress was more a mass meeting and demonstration than a deliberative assembly.[33] Not only did 1084 delegates and "observers" take part, but the proceedings were held in a large hall that prevented anything resembling a debate of issues. The Communists planned the proceedings very skillfully. The Russian and East European delegates were, for the most part, kept in the background, with the Communist delegates from the colonial countries leading the attack on the Western countries. The "colonial question" and the "peace campaign" were the two outstanding issues. Any approach to these issues that differed from the Communist position was dismissed immediately as "insincere." The non-Communist delegates were put into a position in which refusal to support the IUS campaigns *against* colonialism or *for* peace was interpreted to mean action *in favor of* colonialism and *against* peace.

The Communists used dramatic scenes to channel the emotions of the delegates. In a long and stormy demonstration, American "aggression" in Korea was attacked and the appearance of several North Korean "delegates"— military officers in uniform—applauded. Another tumultuous outbreak occurred against British suppression of "democratic" elements in Malaya. A reasoned explanation of the U. S. position—support for IUS objectives, but disagreement on the means by which the IUS was pursuing these aims—got nowhere. A British attempt to read their fact-filled statement combating Communist charges of Western warmongering, and showing up the Soviet position, was continuously interrupted by boos and hisses. Large contingents of "observers," present as representatives of Communist groups in Britain and other countries represented by non-Communist student organizations, took a hand in the proceedings. These "observers" would take the floor in the name of the "democratic" students of their country, to protest statements made by the non-Communist speakers.

Despite this massive attack on the non-Communists at the Prague Congress, they were still not expelled and the façade of unity remained, even though it no longer had any substance.

In fact, during the years after 1948 most of the non-Communist elements had left the WFDY and the IUS, and organized their own international youth and student organizations.[34] In addition to those that left the IUS after the Czech coup, by the spring of 1952 the Norwegian, British, Belgian, French, Canadian, Australian, Brazilian,

Danish, and Scottish national student organizations had withdrawn. As the cold war developed and the intentions of the Communists became clear, the post-war euphoric atmosphere of hope and desire for unity changed rapidly. The idealistic but politically naïve emphasis on unity, which had enabled the Communists to win control of post-war efforts to establish international youth and student co-operation, soon gave way to a better understanding of the realities of the post-war world. Disillusionment was gradually brought to a head by the increasingly partisan nature of the WFDY and the IUS, the events in Czechoslovakia, and the expulsion of the Yugoslavs.

In August 1949 the World Assembly of Youth (WAY) was founded at a conference in Brussels to unite in voluntary cooperative activities the various national youth organizations in a number of the non-Communist countries. Since then the organization has expanded considerably, especially in Asia and Africa, and is today the largest general international youth organization, working with specialized international youth groups such as the Boy Scouts' World Committee, the International Union of Socialist Youth, the International Union of Young Christian Democrats, the International Youth Hostel Federation, the Junior Red Cross, the World Alliance of YMCAs, and the World Association of Girl Guides and Girl Scouts for the improved welfare of the world's young people.

Representatives of student groups still in the IUS, but in the non-Communist minority, and those of student organizations that had disaffiliated from the IUS, had also met in London in December 1949 to air their grievances against the IUS and to decide on a course of action. This meeting listed the following complaints:

1. Overemphasis by the IUS on political questions.
2. The partisan political analyses of the IUS.
3. Its inefficiency in practical activities to aid students.
4. The frequent use of practical activities for political purposes.
5. Its increasingly unrepresentative character.

6. Repeated breaches of the Constitution.
7. The settlement of fundamental issues outside the Council.
8. The uncompromising attitude to any opposition.
9. Its neglect of minorities.[35]

As an aftermath, in December 1950 representatives of twenty-one national student unions met in Stockholm and founded the International Student Conference (ISC), but this was not considered by its founders as a permanent international student organization. Not until the summer of 1952 did the non-Communist student organization decide at a conference in Edinburgh to make the ISC a more permanent organization by establishing a Coordinating Secretariat (COSEC) with headquarters in Leiden, Holland.

These developments almost automatically foredoomed to failure the "unity campaigns" that were conducted by the IUS during 1951 and 1952. In fact, at a "unity meeting" staged in Bucharest in the summer of 1952 only one non-Communist student organization was represented. The IUS Council session that year had representatives from only forty-seven countries as against sixty-one in 1951.

Thus during the years 1945 to 1953 the Communists had succeeded in capturing the organizations initially created to establish international youth and student cooperation. Soon, however, the increasingly partisan nature of the WFDY and IUS alienated the youth organizations of non-Communist countries so that by 1953 the claims of these two bodies to speak for world youth had become obvious fictions. Yet in that same year the death of Stalin brought a retreat from the rigid positions that the Communists had adopted earlier and the development of new lines of policy toward students and youth that were destined to save the IUS and WFDY from atrophy and to make them once more into useful instruments of Communist infiltration and advance.

4/Chapter
The Youth aud Student Fronts Under Khrushchev (1953 — 1964)

The World Federation of Democratic Youth and the International Union of Students followed the general change in tactics introduced gradually into all the Communist front organizations after the death of Stalin in March 1953. The failure of Stalin's foreign policy in the years preceding his death had left the Soviet Union isolated. The new Soviet leaders took steps to emerge from this self-imposed isolation. With the rise of Khrushchev to power, a new approach to world problems was introduced.[1] Violence and the threat of force, major Stalinist tactics, were rejected as unprofitable and dangerous—at least *outside* the Soviet sphere of influence. Not only did Khrushchev reorient the main thrust of Soviet foreign policy —toward the developing lands in Asia, Africa, and Latin America—but he also decided to pursue his objectives by political, economic, and cultural means rather than by violence. In these new circumstances, the front organizations were reshaped in order to bring them out of the isolation resulting from their polemical partisanship. Vituperation and bitter antagonism were replaced by moderation and an appearance of reasonableness.

NEW APPROACHES

It was the IUS that took the lead in developing the new line, and that has achieved the greatest success. The WFDY has lagged behind, and has attained nowhere near the success of the IUS. The first signs of the new moderation in Communist youth and student activities were evident at the IUS Congress in Warsaw in August 1953, at which several Western student organizations, including the British NUS, had representatives.[2] The usual violent demonstrations against the West were absent. The Main Resolution, while polemical in nature, was relatively mild and colorless. The Yugoslavs were invited to attend, an invitation that, however, they did not accept.

The Congress recognized that the openly Communistic nature of the IUS was driving away many potential supporters. The requirement of full membership and of strict discipline in the implementation of the established policies and programs was alienating those non-Communists willing to cooperate with the Communists in certain specific functions or in furtherance of particular issues, but not willing to accept Communist discipline. A further irritant was the membership in the IUS of small, distinctly unrepresentative, Communist-dominated or -influenced student groups that were often in conflict with their respective national student organizations. Hence the IUS now decided to sacrifice these sham groups in the hope of securing cooperation from the more significant national student bodies.[3] Most of the obviously unrepresentative Communist student groups were, accordingly, eliminated from the IUS during the next several years and the IUS revised its membership requirements to provide for an "associate" category that enabled student groups to participate only in those activities in which they were interested.

The Fourth IUS Congress, held during August-September 1956 in Prague, further modified the Constitution to make it more acceptable to non-Communists.[4] Strict centralized control was relaxed to provide some autonomy for affiliated organizations, probably in deference to Asian,

African, Middle Eastern, and Latin American groups from countries where newly won independence had not created a mood favoring rigid ties to an organization obviously controlled by one of the Great Powers. The Constitution was changed to make the highest governing body an *International* Student Congress rather than a *World* Student Congress, and an amendment was adopted that said only that "... the IUS [is] an important organization representing students ...."[5] The IUS also disaffiliated from the WFDY at the Prague Congress and has since followed a policy of accepting only one student organization from each country as a full member.

The first new adherent to the IUS under the revised constitutional provisions was the important British NUS, which re-entered the IUS as an associate member in April 1954 while several other associate members were acquired by 1956. The IUS also sent delegations and representatives to many countries in Europe, Asia, the Middle East, and Latin America,[6] and thereby undertook to compete with the ISC for new adherents from the developing and newly independent nations.

At first the IUS had little success in coming out of its isolation. Its former hostility toward the nationalist movements in the colonial and former colonial countries remained an obstacle to cooperation. The prestige of Communist front organizations was also gravely damaged by the Hungarian revolt in the fall of 1956, although this setback was somewhat offset by Communist support for Egypt against British, French, and Western "imperialism" at the time of the Suez invasion.

Yet even before the crucial year 1956 the newly independent, anti-imperialist states were providing a fertile field where the IUS could expand both its membership and influence. Directing its militantly anti-colonialist appeals especially to the more radical student elements in this "third area," the IUS attacked the ISC and accused it of pretense in its anti-colonial stands.

Nevertheless the rising influence of the IUS was not reflected in any significant increase in membership until after 1960 when the IUS could legitimately claim only ten representative national student unions from non-bloc countries. Yet by November 1961 this number had increased to 25,[7] no doubt because of growing pro-Castro strength among students in Latin America, as well as a generally heightened radicalism among non-Communist students elsewhere. Both the IUS and the WFDY also profited at this time by the adoption among neutralist student and youth groups of the so-called "two bloc" theory, which suggested that true non-alignment justified parallel membership in youth organizations affiliated with the East and West respectively and thus opened the door to new rivalries between Communist bodies and their democratic counterparts.

The competition that developed between the ISC and the IUS for leadership in the international student movement did, of course, indicate an acceptance by the IUS of the fact that it was no longer the only international student organization. The IUS thus abandoned its claim to universality and sought instead to isolate its opposition by increasing its influence in the large and increasingly important neutralist world. The struggle for "unity," however, was not wholly abandoned. Instead of issuing peremptory demands that all student organizations join with the IUS, the latter cultivated an attitude of reasonableness toward the ISC. As the Soviet government sought to adopt a less aggressive foreign policy, so also did the Communist front organizations take steps to renew relations with their non-Communist counterparts.

A representative of the IUS attended the Fourth International Student Conference in Istanbul in early 1954 "to show good will to those seeking cooperation."[8] He spent much time lobbying among delegates who favored negotiating with the IUS on the question of unity. In August 1954, the annual meeting of the IUS Council in Moscow, to which the British, Scottish, and Canadian national student unions sent observers, outlined the steps to be taken in pursuit of the new line:

1. The IUS leadership was to send observers to all meetings where the "international cooperation of students" could be discussed.
2. Cooperation with the World Student Christian Federation, the World Union of Jewish Students, the International Student Movement for the U.N., and other non-Communist student organizations that placed a strong emphasis on attempts to achieve unity and cooperation of all student organizations was to be increased and established on a regular basis when possible.
3. The Executive Committee was to continue to work to reach agreements with national student organizations not yet members of the IUS for the IUS.[9]

The Moscow Council session also called on the Executive Committee to extend its efforts in two special areas where the IUS was attempting to develop cooperation with non-Communists—student sports activities and student relief work.[10] The International University Sports Federation (FISU) had been organized in 1948 to conduct international student sports activities after it had become clear to non-Communists that the IUS was under Communist domination, while the Communists conducted their student sports activities through the Physical Education and Sports Department (PESD) of the IUS. The PESD sponsored a series of annual "World University Summer Games," but since these were unrepresentative, the IUS now sought to reunite the student sports activities and to extend overtures to the FISU in hopes of effecting a United Front. The games scheduled for the summer of 1954, therefore, were postponed in the hope of reaching agreement with the FISU.

The FISU had agreed in August 1953 to hold joint games, but only under conditions that would have made it difficult for the IUS to exercise undue influence. Participation would have been reserved to national student organizations that were recognized by the various national Olympic committees, and this would have eliminated virtually all Communist influence during the preparations in non-Communist countries. The IUS proposal that the two groups meet as equals—invitations to go to all IUS and all FISU members and all national student organizations not members of the FISU or the IUS—was rejected by the FISU. The IUS in turn rejected the FISU conditions since they would have excluded both Communist China and East Germany, but called nevertheless for continued efforts to arrange joint activities with the FISU.[11]

Negotiations in which French, Italian, and Yugoslav student sports organizations played a prominent part ensued during the following years and resulted in the inauguration in 1959 of International University Games, which were held in Rome under Italian sponsorship. By this time student organizations in the Communist countries of Eastern Europe had joined FISU on the latter's terms.[12] Biannual games have been held since then in 1961 in Sofia, and in 1963 in Porto Alegre, Brazil.

Another area of interest to the IUS was that of student relief work. It had carried out such activities through a Student Needs and Welfare Department and an "autonomous" student relief organization—International Student Relief (ISR)—but decided in 1954 to cooperate with World University Service (WUS), a non-political student relief organization that had been formed in 1950.

The IUS had been a member of a predecessor student relief organization, and the founding conference of the WUS had thus left three seats in its General Assembly open for the IUS; an invitation to the IUS to become a sponsoring organization was renewed every year by the WUS General Assembly. To indicate its commitment to universality, WUS even made $2500 available in 1953 for IUS-sponsored student relief.

Nevertheless until the change in Communist tactics after 1953 the IUS preferred to remain outside the World University Service and to operate through International Student Relief, mainly in Eastern Europe and China, areas that were not open to the WUS.

Now, following the new line, the IUS Secretariat decided in 1954 to accept the WUS offer of seats in the General Assembly. A three-man delegation was sent to the WUS General Assembly in Oxford in the summer of 1954 and IUS called on the ISR to discuss conditions under which the two organizations (WUS-ISR) could cooperate in international student relief work.[13]

The WUS generally welcomed the IUS decision but continued formation of IUS committees in competition with existing WUS committees caused much doubt as to the sincerity of the IUS. Indeed at the meeting of the WUS Executive Committee in Geneva in May 1955, the IUS representative indicated that acceptance of the proffered seats did not mean that IUS supported all the activities and policies of the WUS. The IUS reserved the right to disassociate itself from WUS projects it did not support, and would continue its own independent relief activities, primarily through the ISR.

The WUS General Assembly therefore did not renew its invitation to the IUS to take up its allotted seats, and relations between the WUS and the IUS have since remained limited to a mutual exchange of observers at annual meetings.

Here again was an instance of the contradiction in many of the Communist "united front" activities that has plagued all aspects of the movement since the early 1920s. On the one hand the Communists call for "unity" and cooperation, but their unwillingness to implement this policy in practice has continually frustrated the basic motive behind the "united front" policy, which is the desire to expand Communist influence among the mass of non-Communists. Here it meant a desire to have the Communist IUS extend its influence through the gratitude and prestige accruing from student relief activities, especially in the developing countries. Little, if anything, however, has been accomplished by the IUS, and the ISR seems to have been virtually inactive in recent years, at least outside the Communist countries.

The general campaign for "unity" in the international

student movement nevertheless continued in other areas. Specifically, the IUS sought to have ISC-COSEC recognize the existence of two equal student "blocs." In March 1955 the IUS Executive Committee called for a "Conference on Cooperation" to be held in 1956 that would discuss: (1) cooperation in meeting the economic problems that affect students; (2) the introduction of joint faculty activities; (3) the responsibility of the international student movement toward students in developing countries; and (4) problems of student exchanges.[14] This proposal was directed to the Coordinating Secretariat of the International Student Conference, with the request that the next ISC, to which the IUS would send representatives, discuss it. At the same time that this proposal was made, the oft-used technique of the "open letter" was directed to all students urging the maximum degree of cooperation.[15]

In July 1955 the ISC rejected the IUS overture and the concept of two "blocs."[16] Taking the initiative away from the IUS, the ISC indicated, however, that all national student organizations would be invited to the next meeting, including organizations in the Communist countries.

This decision by the ISC was not made with complete unanimity. Considerable differences of opinion existed as to the proper way in which to respond to the IUS overtures. The desire for student unity has been an important consideration ever since 1945, and up to the Soviet intervention in Hungary the European student unions in the ISC had for the most part supported the view that the ISC must treat all IUS overtures seriously. These organizations were leaders in efforts to try to come to some sort of accord with the IUS. The Latin Americans, on the other hand, were very much anti-IUS, but just as European sentiment began to swing over to their side as a result of Soviet actions in Hungary the growing influence of student unions from the "third area" again worked to encourage effort toward unity.

As was to be expected, an IUS Council session in 1955 formally rejected the ISC proposal that student organizations which were members of the IUS attend the next ISC congress, but it did support proposals for cooperation by individual national student organizations and later joined forces with the French student organization (UNEF) in offering a proposal for a "conference of cooperation" that would be convened by a neutral student organization, and would deal only with "practical matters." Taking a beguilingly open attitude, the IUS admitted that it could not expect to succeed in uniting the students of the world by itself:

> Today it is difficult and unrealistic to believe that the unity of the students of the world can be obtained solely by the action of one or the other of the existing international organizations whose duty, in our opinion, lies in facilitating cooperation. We therefore state that a conference of cooperation should be organized on the basis of new principles.[17]

Here again was an attempt to develop cooperation on the basis of two "blocs" in the international student world, but even this overture received a negative response from the majority in the ISC, which was not willing to accord the IUS an unwarranted degree of prestige by cooperating with it on an equal footing. The struggle in the developing lands for student support was going on and would continue to go on regardless of what the IUS might agree to in the way of joint action, and the ISC majority did not want to make membership in a Communist student organization or even cooperation with the Communists on the national or local level an accepted or respectable position.

Less active than the IUS in pursuing "unity" efforts, the WFDY, following the Heads of Government meeting in Geneva in July 1955, nevertheless utilized the "spirit of Geneva" and joined other front organizations in calls for cooperation. The WFDY Secretariat appealed for a relaxation of international tensions in the "Geneva spirit" on the occasion of the tenth anniversary of the founding of the WFDY. In December 1955 the WFDY President called for "fraternal collaboration" in the form of a joint meeting of all international youth organizations. But these appeals, like others, fell on definitely unresponsive ears.

These continued efforts of the IUS and the WFDY to arrange for cooperation with ISC-COSEC, WAY, and other non-Communist organizations were badly hurt by the Hungarian revolt in October-November 1956 and the ruthless Soviet military intervention that was needed to suppress it. The revolt demonstrated more than ever the oppressive character of Communist rule in Eastern Europe and the almost total lack of popular support for a regime that, since coming to power, had depended almost wholly on police terror and coercion to sustain itself. From the IUS and WFDY standpoint matters were made even worse by the fact that students and young workers were, throughout Hungary, in the vanguard of the uprising. Indoctrination, therefore, had failed precisely in the area the Communists considered most crucial. Very much as in the mid-summer rioting in the Polish industrial city of Poznan, so again on a much larger and more impressive scale in Hungary it was the young workers who came forth with demands, not only for better living and working conditions, but for a return to democratic procedures and values. Likewise Hungarian university students protested not so much against material hardships as against Communist curbs on intellectual, artistic, and literary freedom, as well as against the forced isolation that had made free association with the outside world impossible.

All this not only showed general opposition to Communism, but was a repudiation by the rank-and-file of the official claims made by the IUS and WFDY leadership regarding the support these organizations enjoyed even within the Soviet orbit. After the return of Wladyslaw Gomulka to power in Poland and the reassertion in that country of a significant degree of national independence, Polish youth and student organizations also became outspokenly critical of the WFDY and the IUS. Vainly they tried to have the WFDY Secretariat issue a statement of solidarity with Hungarian youth instead of adopting the official propaganda line, which ascribed the revolt to the work of "reactionaries" and "fascists." Polish students also complained that they had been unable to exercise any influence on the policies of the IUS. Throughout the spring and early summer of 1957 these students enjoyed considerable freedom of action, which often expressed itself in demands for greater autonomy both from the government and from the Soviet-sponsored international youth organizations.

Ironically, however, the effect of the East European upheavals of 1956 on the Communist-dominated student and youth organizations was rather short-lived. Having left Hungarian youth to its tragic fate and confined themselves only to statements on the Anglo-French-Israeli invasion of Egypt, they soon resumed their campaign to broaden contact with non-Communist groups and to increase their own respectability and influence.

An unsuccessful attempt was made by the WFDY to get support from WAY and IUSY for a joint campaign against nuclear weapons tests. The IUS-sponsored seminar on International Student Cooperation, meeting in Romania in August 1957, came out in support of a wider and broader meeting, including the principal non-Communist international youth and student organizations.

On October 31-November 1, 1957, representatives of the YM-YWCA and WFDY met informally in Geneva to discuss the question of peace, methods of action to attain peace, and the development of youth activities in the developing countries, but a mutual understanding of the clearly opposite viewpoint held by the participants seems to have been the only result.[18]

A distinction must, however, be made here between the different meanings that the Communists have given to the word "unity" at various times. Up to 1953-1954 the concept meant subordination of all student and youth groups to Communist organizations. For the next several years, unity meant cooperation between the IUS and the ISC, and the WFDY and its non-Communist counterparts. Since about 1958 the Communists have utilized the term "unity" in the international student movement primarily to connote organic union between the IUS and the ISC within one world student organization. Proposals designed to bring this about have been made and repeated by the IUS ever since 1958, but the IUS also continues to talk of cooperation between the IUS and the ISC to facilitate world student unity. Thus while striving for the ultimate goal of one international student organization, which they hope to dominate, the Communists still advocate less ambitious steps in the direction of "cooperation."

The project for organic unity was first launched at the Sixth IUS Congress in Peking in September 1958, where a Round Table Conference on world student unity was proposed. Subsequently, fruitless negotiations took place between the IUS and COSEC on the holding of such a conference. Indeed, ISC-COSEC has not rejected the unity principle, nor does it reject a broad meeting to discuss it. The ISC majority believes, however, that a careful consideration of basic principles is necessary before any new organization can hope to succeed. The IUS, on the other hand, continues to reject any attempt to decide on the principles of unity *before* preparations for a Round Table Conference get under way. It proposes instead the creation of an International Preparatory Committee limited to a discussion of technical questions, which the ISC majority sees merely as a maneuver to stampede its own membership into a new organization on a basis that would enable the Communists to exercise a dominant influence.

At the World Youth Forum in Moscow in the summer of 1961, the informal discussions on world student unity and a Round Table Conference, which had been going on for some time within international student circles, were continued by the Student Commission. The IUS speaker attacked COSEC for not working with IUS toward unity, and this led to a discussion of the whole question of student unity. All opinions were heard, but no meeting of minds emerged.

In the spring of 1962 the IUS sent a letter on the question of a Round Table Conference to all national student organizations participating in the Tenth International Student Conference at Quebec in June-July 1962. Pending agreement on convocation of a conference, the letter proposed that certain activities be jointly sponsored by the IUS and ISC-COSEC "to create the best atmosphere preceding the actual agreement on organizational unity." Suggested projects for joint action were celebration of the victory of the Algerian revolution, a Day of Solidarity with the Cuban revolution, an "international student campaign for general, complete, and controlled disarmament," and an international solidarity campaign with Indonesian students for the "liberation" of West New Guinea. The Seventh IUS Congress in Leningrad in 1962 adopted a resolution on cooperation and unity that endorsed the position set forth in the circular letter of the previous spring. Later still the IUS Executive Committee, meeting in Algiers in May 1963, issued an "Open Letter on International Student Cooperation and Unity," appealing to all student organizations to encourage efforts to form a preparatory committee to arrange for a Round Table Conference.

Meanwhile the WFDY and the IUS had moved their unity efforts to Africa for the first time. The Federation of the Students of the Maghreb (Morocco, Algeria, Tunisia) organized an International Seminar on Student Unity in Tunis that had the support of both ISC-COSEC and the IUS. The two international organizations were to be represented only by observers, but eight members of the IUS Secretariat in Prague were given full delegate status as representatives of their national student organizations. A group of 12 non-Communist delegates supporting the ISC-COSEC withdrew when the IUS delegates refused to accept the principle that in future meetings ISC-COSEC and IUS functionaries should not participate as delegates. The meeting did underline the increasing importance of African student organizations as leaders of the "third world," with the stimulus to leadership in the North African countries being provided by the struggle against French colonial rule, and in Black Africa by the increasing competition between ISC-COSEC and the IUS for African favor. With both organizations providing funds for the international representation of African student organizations, these groups have taken advantage of the opportunity to press their views in the various international forums.

In the North African countries, student organizations were first formed before independence, while in sub-Saharan Africa their formal birth usually followed independence, although organizations of students studying abroad had long been in existence functioning as radical groups whose members are often alienated from, and hostile to, the new nationalist regimes in their homeland as well as to colonial administrations.

Where the Latin American student movement in the period before 1959 tended to exhibit a high degree of homogeneity, the Africans have rapidly split into blocs. Generally the English-speaking student organizations from the former British colonies have joined the ISC and adhere to the traditional Western concept of an apolitical, welfare-oriented student movement. None belonged to the IUS until 1960, and all tend to be critical of the IUS. The French-speaking student organizations, on the other hand, are for the most part not only political, but radical. The Tunisian and Algerian student organizations, which have become two of the most politically important ones since 1956, have set the pattern for the "two bloc" concept of neutrality.[19] This split was already evident at the first Pan-African Student Conference in Kampala, Uganda, in 1958 during the heyday of pan-Africanism under Ghana's Kwame Nkrumah, and developed into a clear break at the second conference the following year. Moreover, it preceded the political division of the new African countries into Casablanca (radical) and Monrovia (moderate) groupings, but where the student split is on clearly linguistic lines the diplomatic division cuts across the language barrier. In these circumstances it is hardly surprising that the IUS has continued to emphasize and expand its activities in Africa. Pressure, within both the

ISC and the IUS, from the student organizations—Communist and non-Communist—of the "third world" will be crucial in shaping the future of the international student movement. In fact, if they came to dominate it, which is not at all impossible, some of the following developments could well occur:

1. A world student organization under Communist influence in which all but a few of the non-Communist student organizations in the West are joined.

2. A new organization, including all of the national student organizations, in which the "third area" groups exercise dominant influence, with both the Communists and the Western student organizations in subordinate positions.

3. The breaking away of the "third area" students to form their own international organization, leaving the ISC and the IUS as relatively small Western and Communist organizations.

4. The formation of a pro-Chinese international student organization, which could split the "third area" groups four ways: pro-China, pro-Soviet, pro-West, and "neutral two bloc."

Another interesting possibility might eventuate from an IUS leadership decision—should the Chinese form a viable student international—to join the ISC on the latter's terms, hoping to gain influence over its policy by leading the "third area" organizations.

WORLD YOUTH FORUM

In early 1960 the IUS and the WFDY tried a new device to rally young people behind Soviet policy objectives. With the easing of international tensions after Premier Khrushchev's visit to the United States in September 1957 and the Communist-generated "spirit of Camp David," it was felt that "conditions are most favorable for a large-scale, frank and interesting discussion" between youth of all countries on the "fate of modern youth." Preparations for such a "discussion" were undertaken by an Organizing Committee in Moscow.[20] Welcome at what the Communists called the World Youth Forum would be representatives of international, national, and local organizations, as well as "specialists." The main themes were to be "Youth, Understanding, Cooperation, and Peaceful Coexistence," "Youth Struggle Against Colonialism and Imperialism for National Independence and Problems of World Peace," and "Youth and Progress."

The organizers invited all of the non-Communist international youth and student organizations to participate, but WAY and most of its national affiliates refused to attend. The IUSY also refused, since it felt that not only Western imperialism but Communist imperialism should be discussed. It demanded that suppression of democratic rights in Eastern Europe and Tibet, and the right of youth in these countries to form independent youth organizations, be included in the agenda.

Nevertheless the World Youth Forum was held in Moscow, from July 25 to August 3, 1961, as a miniature youth festival.[21] The proceedings were primarily in the form of seminars and discussions, but although the sponsors had striven for an appearance of respectability and wide non-partisan support, the forum was little more than an agitational meeting for Communist youth, or for their sympathizers. The professed desire for friendly cooperation was belied by violent attacks on IUSY, ISC-COSEC, WAY, and other non-Communist youth and student organizations.

In traditional style, Communists or sympathizers were represented in every delegation and were always the most active members. The Communist technique of making no distinction between delegates and "observers" further distorted the composition of national delegations with the result that individual speakers were often depicted as representing all the youth of their respective countries, despite the fact that the given speaker did not actually

speak for the national student organization at all. Furthermore, the leaders of the meeting attempted to associate
the non-Communist observers with the decisions taken,
thus giving the appearance of universality. Despite the
fact that the Burmese government refused passports to the
national delegation because of its partisan composition
and the nature of the meeting itself, the organizers of the
Forum claimed that a "widely representative Burmese
delegation" attended. Propaganda on the Forum also
stated that a large and representative Indian youth organization, the Indian Youth Congress, fully supported the
gathering, and the Organizing Committee listed the
Indian Youth Congress as one of its member groups. In
fact, the IYC never sent a representative to the Organizing Committee, and it was only just before the Forum
opened that it was admitted by the sponsors that the
IYC would not attend. Similarly, the British NUS, which
had merely asked for information on the planned meeting,
was elevated to a "supporter" of the project.

Free discussion did take place on many issues, but it
became one-sided due to the limited number of representatives of the Western point of view. The sheer number of
Communist critics tended to overwhelm the Western delegates. In addition, the manner in which the sessions were
conducted acted to inhibit really honest discussion. Pre-
selected delegates gave opening statements or "reports,"
both at the opening session and in the commission meetings. These "reports" were long, and each of the 15 commissions very large; hence little time remained for debate.
Each delegate dwelt on his own national problems and
there was no open give-and-take designed to reach agreement on issues or to narrow the problems needing attention. A façade of "agreement" was provided only by the
organizers, who prepared the final resolutions. One of
these, on youth and disarmament, called for the conclusion
of a "peace treaty with the two German governments, the
purpose of which would be . . . to curb the West German
revenge-seekers and to normalize the situation in West
Berlin."[22] Another, on rural youth, stated that foreign

military bases should be dismantled because they took good land away from the peasants. This was clearly an appeal to wide audiences in countries such as Japan, where military bases have sometimes created difficult local political and social problems. The Forum also came out in support of the World Youth Festival then in preparation for Helsinki in the summer of 1962.

A proposal was made at a WFDY-sponsored "Peace Conference" in Florence, in February-March 1964 for another World Youth Forum, to be "devoted to questions of developing solidarity with the youth and peoples of countries which are fighting for national independence and against colonialism and neo-colonialism."[23] The same Soviet-led "preparatory committee" that made the preliminary arrangements for the first Forum was again set to work, and an International Preparatory Committee was formed again to give the façade of respectability. The Forum, which took place in Moscow in September 1964, was in many ways a success for the Soviets. The approval given to the Soviet line, even by some representative organizations from the developing countries, was an indication of the success of Soviet propaganda. The establishment of an International Solidarity Fund, designed to aid youth and students in the developing countries, is possibly an important opportunity for its administratiors (WFDY-IUS) to win prestige among the African, Asian and Latin American youth and students. (An International Solidarity Bund had been established earlier to facilitate the attendance of sympathizing young people from the colonial and newly independent areas at the World Youth Festivals. The purposes of this new ISF are considerably broader.) A disrupting note at the second World Youth Forum was the bitter public clash between Soviet and Chinese spokesmen and their respective supporters. More will be said about this confrontation below.

In pursuing their new policy of ostensible cooperation after 1953, both the WFDY and the IUS sought to have their consultative status with the United Nations Economic and Social Council (ECOSOC) and the United Nations

Educational, Scientific, and Cultural Organization (UNESCO) restored. Both of these bodies make provision for granting consultative status to non-governmental international organizations so that these U.N. activities can benefit from cooperation with the more important international professional, technical, scientific, and service organizations. The WFDY was originally accorded category B status[24] by ECOSOC in March 1947, but its attempt at the following session to establish a closer tie with ECOSOC by requesting category A status was rejected. Later the increasingly partisan nature and political character of the WFDY led to its loss of consultative status altogether, when at the eleventh session of ECOSOC in July-August 1950 it was placed on the register of non-governmental international organizations with which the ECOSOC merely consults on an *ad hoc* basis.[25] The IUS evidently never even applied for ECOSOC recognition.

UNESCO accepted both the WFDY and the IUS as consultative organizations in February 1949, but consultative status was revoked from both in December 1952 since their activities had ceased to accord with the basic principles of UNESCO.[26] Both organizations were placed on the register of organizations with which the Director-General maintains informal relations.

Both the WFDY and the IUS, however, continued to cooperate where possible in UNESCO-sponsored activities. In September 1957 the WFDY sent an observer to the meeting of the World Federation of Associations for the United Nations and along with several other Communist front organizations reapplied for consultative UNESCO status in the same year. Nevertheless the Tenth General UNESCO Conference in November 1958 refused to renew the consultative status of either organization despite a Soviet threat to withdraw financial support from UNESCO.

Most recently, the Communists participated in the first International Conference of Youth sponsored by UNESCO in Grenoble, France, in August-September 1964, a conference primarily of delegates from the UNESCO member countries rather than from youth organizations as such. One of the six conference vice-chairmen was Yuri Kharlamov, president of the U.S.S.R. Student Council. This meeting did little to further the WFDY or the IUS, but it did provide an opportunity for Communist youth and student representatives to participate and expound their views in a non-partisan forum.

AFRICA AND ASIA

This effort to re-establish contact with bodies of the United Nations and with non-Communist organizations generally was closely related to the sharp rise in Soviet concern with African, Asian, Middle Eastern, and Latin American affairs. Stalin's almost wholly negative attitude toward indigenous nationalist movements had been abandoned by 1955 and gave way instead to Soviet backing of the Bandung Conference and an exchange of visits between Soviet, Indian, and Burmese heads of state. Close relations were also established with Egypt and Indonesia and overtures made to the world's dependent areas under the banner of "anti-colonialism."

The new approach was reflected in the programs of all Communist front organizations. As early as February 1955 an International Day Against Colonialism had been organized with WFDY backing.

The Anglo-French-Israeli invasion of Suez in November 1956 occasioned a spate of attacks on Western colonialism and demonstrations of "solidarity" with the local nationalist movements. In early 1958 the IUS and the WFDY announced their support for Algerian youth, for students in Cyprus and the Cameroons, for Indonesia's claims to West New Guinea, and for Cuban student resistance to U. S. "aggression." The IUS also called upon all member organizations to assure that places for Asian, African, and Latin American students were made available at the universities in their respective countries.

This latter endeavor has come to occupy an important, if dubiously successful, part in Communist youth and student activities. In recent years more and more students from non-Western areas have been brought for study in the Soviet Union and the East European countries. In 1960 Friendship University, dedicated to the memory of Patrice Lumumba, was opened in Moscow, and other specialized institutions for "third area" students have been started elsewhere in the bloc.

The IUS has not limited itself to encouraging the training of young Asians, Africans, and Latin Americans. During the first half of 1958 an IUS program of training African students in political and paramilitary activities got under way in Prague. About 250 young Africans, most of them from universities in Western Europe, began a three-year course designed to produce future Communist organizers and agitators. The process of selection used by the IUS for this cadre training program did not emphasize a belief in Communism as much as it did strong anti-Western attitudes. The best of these students are returned to their homeland before the three years are up, others are posted as instructors in similar schools in the U.S.S.R., while still others are sent as political instructors to training camps for agents destined for Africa.

The WFDY meanwhile aided the first African Youth Festival, held in the Sudan in September 1958, and in December 1958 began to hold some of its meetings outside of Europe; an Executive Committee meeting in Colombo that month was used as a forum to associate the WFDY with the nationalist movements in the colonial countries and as an occasion to express "solidarity with the peoples fighting for independence."[27] The Executive Committee and Bureau met again in Conakry, Guinea, in March 1960 when Communist influence in that West African country was high, while the IUS Executive gathered in Tunis in February 1960 and organized its Congress in Baghdad under the sponsorship of the Kassem regime in the autumn of that year.

The WFDY and the IUS were also behind the First Afro-Asian Conference, held in February 1959 in Cairo.[28] The actual sponsors were the Afro-Asian Peoples' Solidarity Committee and the UAR Youth Welfare Organization, but the Preparatory Committee followed the same objectives as did the IUS-WFDY-dominated International Preparatory Committee preparing for the Seventh World Youth Festival in Vienna.[29]

The presence at this conference of delegates from the U.S.S.R. caused a great deal of controversy. Indonesia, Laos, Thailand, Burma, South Korea, the Philippines, Turkey, and Nationalist China boycotted the conference because the Soviet delegates were not considered Afro-Asian in the terms laid down at the Bandung Conference. South Vietnam appeared, but then withdrew. The Indian, Japanese, and Pakistani delegations agreed that the U.S.S.R. had no place there but decided not to make an issue of its presence.

The conference itself began on the basis of "positive neutrality," but the pro-Communists succeeded in overcoming resistance and won support for their line on imperialism and other issues. The bias of the meeting was evident from such things as its condemnation of the U. S. occupation of Okinawa and its silence over Soviet occupation of the Kuriles, both of which followed Japan's defeat in World War II.

The Sixth IUS Congress in Baghdad in October 1960 was characterized by Iraqi President Kassem, who opened the proceedings, as an opportunity to coordinate the struggle against imperialism.[30] Anti-colonialism provided one of the two main themes of the Congress, the other being disarmament.

The Pan-African Youth Conference planned for January 1962 in Guinea, to form an all-African youth organization, had to be postponed until April because of unrest associated with the abortive Communist attempt to subvert the Guinean government at the end of 1961 in which the Communist-infiltrated Guinean student organization was deeply involved. Still the WFDY and the IUS were both active in preparing for this youth conference, which resulted in a compromise agreement to form a Pan-African Youth Movement, with its seat in Guinea, but with no affiliation with other world or continental youth movements, whether Communist or non-Communist. Observers from both the IUS and WFDY, and ISC-COSEC and WAY, would be present at the headquarters of the new organization,[31] but the basic differences between the radicals and the moderates in the ranks of African youth has remained a serious obstacle to the development of PAYM.

The Communist efforts to infiltrate and capture meetings worked to their disadvantage in the case of the International Seminar Against Colonialism in Algiers in April 1963, following a WFDY demonstration on the occasion of the Communist-sponsored World Youth Day Against Colonialism and for Peaceful Coexistence. Disregard of Africa's real problems in favor of resolutions denouncing U. S. actions in Laos, South Vietnam, and Cuba, plans for a Malaysian federation, and Israel as the principal agent of imperialism in the Middle East alienated most of the delegates. The host Algerian student organization was particularly angry over the way the seminar was turned into a Communist meeting, where the Sino-Soviet quarrel took up much of the time, thus pointing up a dilemma with which the Communist front organizations will be increasingly faced if they persist—as indeed they probably must—in using such meetings, conferences, and seminars as forums for the exposition of current Soviet, or Chinese, foreign policy lines in disregard of the understandable desire of Afro-Asian young people to discuss the real problems of their countries.

LATIN AMERICA

Beginning in 1954, the Communist fronts in general and especially the WFDY began to devote increased attention to Latin America. A South American "Spring Rally" was planned by the WFDY for Santiago, Chile, in the spring of that year, and a Central American and Caribbean Youth Festival for Guatemala in the fall. However, opposition from the Chilean government, and the fall of the Communist-infiltrated Arbenz regime in Guatemala, frustrated these plans.

At the same time the IUS had also sent agitators and organizers to Latin America.[32] In 1953 and 1954 the number of IUS and WFDY delegations to the Latin American countries increased considerably, but despite all efforts only the Ecuadorian student organization maintained its membership in the IUS.

From 1955 on, however, the Communist front organizations met with more success. Taking advantage of the radical reaction by students to the deteriorating social and economic situation in Latin America and the failure of democratic regimes to do much better than the dictatorships of the right, the Communists succeeded in convincing many students that Marxist solutions were the only answer to the grave problems of the area. The success of Castro in Cuba reinforced a growing belief in the need for, and possibility of, radical social revolution. Communist strength in the Latin American student movements soared in the period 1957-1959, and by their skill and activity Communist students were often able to succeed in reaching positions of influence in their national student organizations even though they were not really supported by a majority.

After the Latin American student organizations, basically nationalist and anti-Communist, organized the First Latin American Student Congress in Montevideo, Uruguay, in June 1955, IUS publications began to devote more attention to Latin America.[33] In 1956 an IUS delegation toured several Latin American countries and in succeeding years the IUS supported three full-time traveling representatives in Latin America, began conducting leadership seminars at its headquarters in Prague, and offered travel grants to Latin Americans attending the World Youth Festivals.

These activities of the IUS and the WFDY in Latin America were, however, hampered by the uncooperative, and often hostile, attitude of both national student organizations and the national governments. The large and influential Argentine student union, for instance, wished to retain the freedom it had won after the overthrow of the Peron dictatorship in September 1955. This sentiment was reflected at the Second Latin American Student Congress in La Plata, Argentina, in April 1957, where it was felt that both "Yankee" and Soviet imperialism deserved to be condemned.

Only with the coming into power of Castro in Cuba was the task of Communist front organizations made easier. The Fidelistas worked hard to make their leader into a symbol of anti-U. S. nationalism and also provided a friendly base for conferences and training schools for the Latin American area. In February 1959, at the Eighth International Student Conference in Lima, Peru, it was already quite apparent that pro-Castro forces had become a powerful element in the Latin American student movement and that they were receiving massive support from the WFDY and the IUS, both of which were subsequently to mount a substantial propaganda campaign to prevent Cuba's exclusion from the inter-American system at the OAS Foreign Ministers' Conference at Punta del Este at the beginning of 1962.

Before then, however, a Latin American Youth Congress had been held in Havana in the summer of 1960.[34] The preparations followed the standard Communist front formula. An International Preparatory Committee, with the appearance of widespread support, organized the proceedings so as to assure control by the sponsoring WFDY. The youth affiliates of two non-Communist Venezuelan political parties were persuaded to join the IPC. The motto of the Congress was "For the Liberation of Latin America." A later rallying cry of the Congress was "Yankee Imperialism Is the Greatest Enemy of Latin America."[35]

Despite diligent efforts, however, the Congress proved a failure. Of 1500 expected delegates, only 339 Cubans and others attended. Several delegations withdrew during the Congress, including those of Brazil, Colombia, and Panama, and it was later admitted by the Yugoslav delegate that only left Socialist and Communist youth organizations had actually attended.[36]

Undaunted, the WFDY and the IUS continue to stress activities in Latin America, no less than in Africa. The first Latin American University Games were held in Havana in October 1962 under FISU, Cuban University Federation (FEU), and IUS Sports Council sponsorship. A second Latin American Youth Congress, planned by a newly created Latin-American Commission in the WFDY Secretariat, was held in Santiago, Chile, in March 1964.[37] The two most important Chilean political youth organizations, the Christian Democratic Youth and the Radical Youth, refused to give their support, even though a representative of the latter is a WFDY Vice-President. The Congress was thus left to convene as a sectarian meeting of pro-Communist groups, not all of which were youth groups. A number of Communist-dominated trade unions were represented. The Ecuadorian, Peruvian, Mexican, and some other delegations left the Congress when it became clear that it was a Castro-Communist demonstration. The emphasis was, as expected, on condemning "U. S. imperialism" as the basic reason for lack of economic and social progress in Latin America.

The IUS has also been active in Latin America, particularly in the area of "student welfare." Support was given to the first Central American Seminar on Student Welfare, held in San Salvador, El Salvador, in June 1963 and organized by the El Salvador student organization (AGEUS). WFDY and IUS propaganda has naturally also continued to emphasize support for Cuba. The WFDY Bureau at the end of 1962 declared that solidarity with Cuba "is a steady and highly significant political factor in the action of the WFDY."[38] It called for the mobilization of youth to end the U. S. blockade of Cuba, U. S. aerial surveillance, and "subversive activities" organized against the Cuban government, and for the dismantling of the Guantanamo naval base.

The area of greatest potential success for the Communists in Latin America seems, however, at present to lie

within the ISC, rather than the activities of the IUS or
the WFDY. The Castro-Communist influence in the ISC
continues to be strong, emanating primarily from the
national student unions in Cuba, Uruguay, Argentina,
Peru, Puerto Rico, the Dominican Republic, and until
recently, Brazil and Ecuador. The recent Brazilian crack-
down on Communist organizations, especially the student
organization (UNEB), and the prohibition by the
Ecuadorian government of all existing student organizations (new ones are to be formed only on a clearly non-
political basis), will serve to decrease Communist influence
not only in the ISC but within the Latin American student movement as a whole.

The economic and social unrest in Latin America, as
well as the strong nationalist sentiment in that area; the
rising political and social consciousness and the legacy of
anti-colonialism in black Africa; the general wave of
"rising expectations" throughout the economically less-
developed nations of the world; and the demand for simple
solutions in an ever more complex world will all provide
fertile ground for Communist action. The WFDY and the
IUS will, in the circumstances, certainly continue their
efforts to win youth and students for their causes, on the
one hand encouraging the spread of Marxist ideas so as
to generate empathy with the existing Communist system
and on the other hand attempting to win influence, or
control, over youth in Latin America, Asia, Africa, and
the Middle East by exploiting legitimate grievances and
aspirations. This will probably be done indirectly through
new front organizations formed regionally, under WFDY
and IUS auspices, as these groups continue to put predominant emphasis on their work in the underdeveloped
countries.

RECENT PROPAGANDA THEMES

Despite the emphasis on "peaceful coexistence" in
Soviet foreign policy, the propaganda themes of the front
organizations continue to follow an anti-Western line.

This has been especially so in regard to the key issues that divide the Communist and non-Communist world. Generally, the WFDY has taken a most active and vociferous role in these propaganda efforts, while the IUS adopts a more restrained attitude.

As early as 1954, the front organizations were extremely active in agitating against the European Defense Community. After the defeat of the plan by the French National Assembly, Communist organizations were equally active in opposing the London and Paris Agreements, which permitted West Germany to rearm and enter NATO. The WFDY sponsored a series of conferences and demonstrations and initiated an Anti-EDC European Youth Conference in East Berlin in April 1954. The WFDY-sponsored International Gathering of Rural Youth at the end of 1954 protested against the London and Paris Agreements, which were said to be "reviving militarism" in West Germany. All European youth was called upon to oppose ratification of these agreements "vigorously." The WFDY also made the Fifth World Youth Festival in Warsaw in August 1955 a part of the campaign against German rearmament.

After the failure of Communist attempts to frustrate implementation of the London and Paris Agreements, the campaign against German rearmament merged into the more general campaign against German militarism and atomic war. The Vienna Appeal against atomic warfare issued by the World Peace Council was made a major part of the WFDY propaganda, and signatures were collected among youth for the Appeal. During 1955 the WFDY and the IUS supported all the "ban-the-bomb" campaigns, and while all groups and organizations active in such work were by no means Communist-dominated, the Communists certainly played a major role. The IUS and the WFDY organized a continuous series of meetings and conferences, and issued numerous appeals demanding the end of nuclear weapons tests; the peaceful use of atomic energy; the prohibition of thermonuclear weapons; and disarmament.

In March 1958 the WFDY Executive Committee outlined its three major propaganda themes of that period—
peaceful coexistence, opposition to atomic armament, and
anti-colonialism. Adopting the position of the Soviet
government, it supported the plan for a Summit Conference and called on youth to support the World Peace
Council, the World Congress for Disarmament and Cooperation in Stockholm in July 1958, and the Fourth
World Conference Against Atomic and Hydrogen Weapons, scheduled for Tokyo in August. In May 1958 all the
front organizations acclaimed the Soviet announcement of
the suspension of nuclear weapons tests. The WFDY
Secretariat called on the U. S. and the U. K. to follow
suit, and attacked the West German *Bundestag* decision
to accept atomic-capable weapons from the U. S. In 1962,
however, the WFDY and the IUS were conspicuously
silent when the Soviet Union broke the moratorium on
nuclear testing.

Meanwhile, however, the main themes of the Sixth
IUS Congress in Baghdad in the summer of 1960 were
peace and disarmament, and in September 1960, on the
eve of the UN debate on disarmament, the WFDY Secretariat issued a statement indicating that the U.S.S.R. was
the only government to have taken positive steps to bring
about a reduction in armaments.

The losses in credibility and prestige to the Communist front organizations that resulted from the Soviet
resumption of nuclear tests in 1962 were severe. The first
such setback for the youth and student movement occurred
within the IUS. Previously the large, active, and representative Japanese student union, *Zengakuren*, had been a
noisy and at times violent supporter of the anti-Western
"ban-the-bomb" campaign. With the resumption of nuclear tests by the Soviet Union, however, the *Zengakuren*
lessened its anti-American, "anti-imperialist" policy, and
came out in opposition to Soviet nuclear tests;[39] and when
its delegation to the Seventh IUS Congress in Leningrad
in August 1962, just after the resumption of these tests,
condemned the Soviet Union, heated debates and clashes

with Soviet youth and student bureaucrats ensued. A similar sense of dismay at this abrupt Soviet policy reversal also beset other IUS- and WFDY-affiliated groups, who proved quite as difficult to placate.

By 1963, however, the protests had died down somewhat and the Bureau of the WFDY again issued an appeal "For General Disarmament and Peace" in which it asked for immediate agreement on the cessation of nuclear tests, dismantling of all rocket sites and military bases on foreign soil, and the setting up of atom-free zones in Europe, the Pacific, and Latin America.

Both the WFDY and the IUS have also consistently supported the Soviet position on Germany. Both gave immediate and complete support to the East German regime when it erected the Berlin Wall in August 1961. On May 8, 1963, the anniversary of V-E Day, the WFDY and the IUS arranged a Day of Struggle of Youth and Students Against West German Militarism and Imperialism, where the Adenauer-De Gaulle pact, under which Germany and France formally reconciled their long-standing enmities, was attacked. An appeal was issued on this occasion that asked support for the Soviet position on Germany and called on all youth to demand the:

> Signing of a German peace treaty.
> Transformation of West Berlin into a "Free," neutral city.
> Recognition of East Germany.
> Peaceful coexistence between the two German States.
> Repudiation of the use of force in settling disputes.
> Abolition of West German training bases in Britain and France.
> Inclusion of the two German states in a nuclear-free zone.[40]

The IUS Executive Committee, meeting in Algiers in May 1963, continued the propaganda against German "militarism," and called on the African students to show solidarity with the students and population of both the German Democratic and Federal Republics in the "struggle against

German militarism," and to launch a campaign for the diplomatic recognition of East Germany.

And so it has been in other areas of Soviet interest. When the Arbenz regime was overthrown in Guatemala in 1954, the WFDY protested U. S. "aggression." After the Geneva Conference on Indo-China the same year, it endorsed the Chinese and general Communist position with respect to the settlement. In 1960, it called for an end to UN "intervention" in the Congo, and during 1962-63, after the overthrow and execution of General Kassem in Iraq, its propaganda organs eulogized the fallen pro-Communist leader and attacked the new and much less sympathetic regime.

Continuing efforts are still being made by Communist youth and student organizations to mobilize the world's youth behind the Soviet propaganda campaigns. The international Conference of Youth and Students for Disarmament, Peace, and National Independence, held in Florence, Italy, in 1964, was a recent attempt in this direction.[41] Gathering together representatives of student and youth organizations that for the most part were IUS and WFDY members, the conference passed resolutions concerned with the "end of imperialist aggression in Vietnam," the dismantling of all military bases in Africa, a ban on the spread of nuclear weapons, and efforts to "resolve the Palestine question."

The participation of the WFDY and the IUS in all of these "campaigns," and the orientation of their propaganda, are clear evidence of the role these organizations play in helping to further Soviet foreign policy goals. These fronts remain auxiliary weapons used primarily to make official Communist policy more acceptable and effective, but they are nevertheless important weapons. This is particularly so in the developing countries. The fronts are for the most part clearly identified in Western Europe and the other advanced countries, where Communist-non-Communist divisions are fairly well stabilized. In the new states, however, the situation is different. The fronts make highly charged appeals to leaders and peoples and play on those issues that arouse the highest degree of emotional response—peace, solidarity, national independence, and anti-colonialism. In those areas, youth and student functionaries are working through organizations whose links to overt Communist groups and individuals are less apparent than they are in Europe, and the prevalent lack of political sophistication is an important ally for these disguised Communist activities.

THE SINO-SOVIET SPLIT

The ideological dispute within the world Communist movement, focused on the Sino-Soviet schism, has had serious effects upon the international front organizations in recent years. Dissension has broken out into the open and has impaired the attempts of front organizations to present themselves as broadly supported non-political movements.

The first signs of dissension involved the Chinese and the Yugoslavs, with the former advocating an aggressive policy for the Communist movement, and condemning the independence and "revisionism" of the Yugoslavs. The Chinese student organization at the Fifth IUS Congress in Peking in 1958 already displayed a hostile attitude toward the Yugoslav observer. However, since the Soviet Communist Party was also at odds with the Yugoslavs at this time, the extent of developing Sino-Soviet differences was not immediately apparent: the Soviet-led IUS Executive refused to accept an invitation by the Yugoslav student organization to attend its 1959 Congress.

The IUS Executive Committee session in Tunis in February 1960 was the scene of further Yugoslav-Chinese recrimination. The Yugoslavs supported the policy of the IUS in seeking cooperation with other international student organizations (ISC-COSEC), whereas the Chinese were for a sharp and aggressive break with the "agents of imperialism" and advanced a resolution that was defeated because it "aimed to narrow the initiative of the IUS for international student cooperation."[42] Differences of this kind also emerged at the Sixth IUS Congress in Baghdad in October 1960 but appear to have been kept behind the scenes.

By 1962, however, with the Soviet and Chinese Communist parties in open conflict, differences were no longer muted in the front organizations either, and direct confrontations between representatives of the two countries became sharper and more frequent. In April 1962 the pro-Chinese Albanian youth organization paper, *Zeri i Rinisë*, denounced the "revisionists" in the WFDY who supported peaceful forms of opposition to imperialism, as against armed "national liberation struggle." The Seventh IUS Congress in Leningrad in August 1962 was the first occasion where Sino-Soviet differences were voiced at an international youth or student forum. There was real discussion and give-and-take between the Soviet and Chinese representatives and their respective supporters.

The dispute between the Soviet Union and Communist China has a complex background, and involves many issues. For the front organizations, however, the key question seems to be that of peace versus national liberation and where the emphasis should be placed. As a result a struggle for control of the front organizations has arisen. The Soviet policy position can be summed up as follows: the maintenance of world peace is the most important task for students, and indeed for all mankind; the "imperialists" are forcing the arms race and sabotaging the disarmament talks, yet the "forces of peace," consisting of the U.S.S.R., its Communist supporters, and the neutralists, can by mass action save the peace and force the imperialists to accept agreement on disarmament; the achievement of disarmament will facilitate the struggles for national independence by removing the foreign military bases and troops that assure imperialist and neo-colonialist dominance. The Chinese, on the other hand, reject the implicit Soviet position that the national-liberation struggle depends on disarmament and the maintenance of peace. Peace, to the Chinese, is attainable not only through disarmament but also through active struggle for national liberation from imperialism. The two Communist powers thus differ on the seriousness with which one must view a nuclear war. To the Soviets its avoidance is the most important task of mankind, including the Communist movement. The Chinese, more aggressive and apparently less concerned with the results of a nuclear holocaust, feel that the national-liberation struggle is the most important task, and seem willing to accept a nuclear war if necessary in order to defeat the "imperialists," led, of course, by the United States.

At the Leningrad Congress the Soviet student organization left it to the members of the IUS Secretariat and national organizations supporting the Soviet position to block Chinese attempts to amend the peace resolution so as to emphasize the national-liberation struggle. Supporting the Chinese were delegates from Albania and North Korea and some more radical student organizations from the "third world." These latter groups are generally not interested in problems other than their own and are, perhaps, typified by the General Union of Palestine Students (GUPS), formed from refugee Palestinian Arab students, who are for the most part not particularly Marxist-Leninist oriented, study throughout the world, and have but one concern—the expulsion of the Jews from Israel and a return to what they believe to be their rightful homeland. With such backing as this, the Chinese succeeded in obtaining significant amendments to the Soviet-inspired draft resolution on the peace question, which finally equated national liberation, coexistence, and disarmement as important elements in the fight for world peace.

During 1963 the frequency of these clashes increased considerably. Bitter pro- and anti-Chinese factional quarrels took place at the International Seminar Against Colonialism in Algiers in April 1963, much to the disgust of the African delegates. In July the anti-Chinese Communist student delegates to the WFDY-IUS-sponsored Seminar for Students from Underdeveloped Countries in Brazil supported the Indian delegates when they clashed with the Chinese over the Sino-Indian border dispute.

In the summer of 1963, the WFDY Secretariat, over the opposition of the Chinese representative, sent telegrams to the Foreign Ministers of the U. S., the U. K., and the U.S.S.R. supporting the negotiations then under way for a nuclear test-ban treaty.[43] A bitter quarrel between the Soviet and Chinese representatives apparently took place during the Secretariat meeting at which the telegrams were approved.[44] The All-China Federation of Democratic Youth issued a statement in Peking shortly thereafter condemning the WFDY action, as well as a similar action by the IUS.[45] The East German youth organization responded by accusing the Chinese of trying to split the WFDY.[46]

This accusation seems to have had a good deal of substance. Reports indicate that the Chinese are indeed adopting an obstructive attitude within the WFDY and the IUS. The Chinese delegate to the WFDY Bureau session in late October 1963 opposed the resolution approving cooperation with the Yugoslav Youth League.[47] Within the WFDY Secretariat there also seems to have developed a serious antagonism between the Chinese representative and the Soviet-oriented leadership. Charging the Soviet Komsomol with becoming "decadent," and arguing that they are the only really revolutionary youth organization, the Chinese are trying to persuade delegates from the Asian, African, and Latin American countries that they have no common interests and aims with "the whites."[48]

As they have been doing in other areas, as by the formation of an Afro-Asian Journalists' Association, an Afro-Asian Lawyers' Conference, an Afro-Asian Workers' Conference, and Afro-Asian Writers' Conferences, the Chinese are manifestly trying to form new international youth and student organizations in which they, and not the Russians, will be the dominant force. Supported by the Indonesian government, a sponsoring committee for an Asian, African, and Latin American Students' Conference met in Djakarta in late November 1963.[49] Represented were youth and student organizations from Indonesia,

China, Cuba, Algeria, and Brazil.[50] The meeting disagreed
with the WFDY Bureau on the issue of inviting several
non-Communist youth and student organizations such as
the Indian National Congress Youth, the Socialist Youth
of Japan, youth sections of the Japanese Trade Organization SOHYO, the Afro-Asian Solidarity Council, and the
Pan-African Youth Movement to the Executive Committee
meeting scheduled for Djakarta in December 1963. Having
the support of the Indonesian government, the Indonesian
preparatory committee indicated to the Bureau that visas
to the Executive Committee session would be issued only
with their approval. This open veto over its plans the
Soviet-oriented Bureau refused to accept and therefore
postponed the meeting,[51] which it refused to see held on
Chinese terms. The WFDY did send a delegation to
Indonesia in January 1964 to participate in an International Solidarity Meeting of Youth for the National
Independence of North Kalimantan (North Borneo) and
Against the Neo-Colonialist Plan of Great Malaysia.[52] Its
members apparently discussed their differences with the
Indonesians, but evidently no agreement was reached.

After this "solidarity meeting" the Indonesian Youth
Front and twelve of the delegations formed a Preparatory
Committee for an Afro-Asian Youth Solidarity Organiza-
tion,[53] and plans were to be made for an Asian-African
Youth Conference in Djakarta in April 1964, at which the
new organization would be founded. Represented on the
Preparatory Committee were China, Japan, North Korea,
North Vietnam, the Philippines, Laos, Malaya, "North
Kalimantan," Angola, Zanzibar, and Niger, all of which
could be counted as pro-Chinese elements.[54] Plans are thus
under way for the formation of two new pro-Chinese
organizations—and membership in them is to be limited to
African, Asian, and Latin American groups.

The Chinese still remain inside the IUS and the
WFDY to oppose the pro-Soviet policies of the leaderships
of these two organizations. At the IUS Executive Committee meeting in Budapest (February 12-21, 1964) opposition to the leadership-sponsored resolution supporting the

nuclear test-ban treaty came from seven delegations, including the Chinese, North Korean, North Vietnamese, Japanese, Guadeloupese, and FEANF, with two abstentions.[55] The Chinese representative attacked the Soviet student organization violently for placing disarmament above all else. The Chinese student organization threatened to leave the IUS if it did not return to its traditional stand on fighting imperialism.[56]

A similar Sino-Soviet dispute, especially over support of the test-ban treaty by the WFDY, took place at the meeting of the WFDY Executive Committee when finally held in Budapest (July 10-15, 1964). Further, bitter attacks were made on the Soviet leadership of the WFDY by the Chinese after the meeting. Clear hints of a forthcoming split can be noted in the Chinese statements (Radio Peking, August 4, 1964).

The conflict between the Soviet and Chinese positions was an important factor at the World Youth Forum in September 1964. The Chinese had not attended the IPC meetings, but did show up for the Forum itself. Differences in interpretation of "peaceful coexistence," a Soviet-sponsored effort to embarrass the Chinese by calling for an immediate "liberation" of Hong Kong and Macao, and a proposal that China and India settle their border difficulties by peaceful means (which was interpreted by the Chinese to be Soviet support for India) led to bitter and angry attacks and recriminations.

The Chinese still remain inside both the WFDY and the IUS but have have challeneged Soviet ideological and political guidance of both organizations at their recent meetings. They have made a major issue of these organizations' endorsement of the test-ban treaty and have denounced both bodies for giving support even to this very limited U. S.-Soviet accord. Clashes between Chinese and Soviet-oriented delegations occurred at the March 1964 Latin American Youth Festival and at other meetings of Communist youth meetings on such issues as "the national liberation struggle." In fact, since 1963, the Chinese have worked energetically with the Organization of Indonesian Students (PPMI) to organize a new Afro-Asian-Latin American Student organization as a direct rival to Russian-sponsored youth groups. They have, in fact, gone so far as to sponsor an "Initiating Committee" for this enterprise, which met at Djakarta in November 1963.

The Sino-Soviet differences in the youth and student front organizations seem to be moving towards a split and the formation of rival organizations. The consequences of such a development on the prospects for extension of Communist influence—whether of the Soviet, Chinese or other variety—are difficult to foretell. Certainly the Leningrad Congress of the IUS, and developments since then, have illustrated the difficulties with which the Russians are faced in winning new adherents. The emphasis on peace tends to lead the fronts to direct their chief appeals to the Western European countries. They stress such issues as the German question, atom-free zones in the Baltic and Mediterranean, Soviet disarmament proposals, and peaceful coexistence. The dilemma is that if youth in the Western countries is to support the Soviet position on these issues the IUS and the WFDY must moderate their anti-Western, anti-imperialist propaganda, thereby lessening their appeal to youth in the "third area" countries and increasing the appeal of, and opportunities for, the Chinese. Control of the IUS by the Soviet and other East European student organizations makes certain that it will follow the Soviet line. The dilemma of the IUS, however, is that as it increases its influence by broadening membership to include non-Communist organizations, and not only accepts the right of new members to be heard, but actively seeks their support, it also weakens control over the organization by the Secretariat. The Soviet-led IUS Secretariat had to compromise at the Leningrad Congress for the first time. This may be indicative of the possibility that at some point the "third area" members will come to exercise a deciding influence on their own, and or on China's, behalf.

Thus it seems clear that the situation in the international Communist youth and student movements will get worse before it gets better. As long as the Soviet and the Chinese parties remain in sharp conflict, the prospects for an extension and hardening of the splits within the front organizations remain strong. This will tarnish the already drab image of "universal representation" cultivated by the Communist organizations, if indeed that image has survived the realities of the past fifteen or more years.

5/Chapter
Youth Festivals: Their History and Function

The World Youth Festivals sponsored by the WFDY and the IUS have been a significant part of the propaganda directed by Communists toward young people. Introduced on the initiative of the WFDY, ostensibly "to develop and strengthen international friendship and understanding among youth of all countries,"[1] these festivals were held biannually from 1947 through 1959. The most recent was held in Helsinki, Finland, in July and August of 1962.

The specific objectives of the festivals have included the recruiting of new members for the WFDY and the IUS and their local member organizations, as well as for other front organizations; the development of the festivals as a recognized occasion where the youth of the world can meet, under Communist sponsorship, thus providing an institutionalized means of spreading Communist propaganda among youth; encouragement of the idea that the Communist way of life is the best, and that the U.S.S.R. is the leader in the fight for democracy and peace; and the furthering of the view that the U.S.S.R. is the leading supporter of "oppressed" peoples.

THE CHANGING PATTERN

Since they have been but another instrument of Soviet policy, the festivals must be seen in the context of the international political scene. As Soviet policy has changed, so has the orientation of the festivals. The first of them—in Prague in 1947—was held at a time when Stalin was introducing the "two-camp" theory into Soviet foreign policy and the Communist front organizations. It capitalized on the "anti-fascist" emotionalism and anti-war idealism that had led to the founding of the WFDY and the IUS. Fascism and imperialism were condemned, without being directly defined, and the exhibits, slogans, and demonstrations arranged so that the U. S. was depicted as the archetype of a fascist, imperialist power while the Soviet Union was seen to be for peace and the well-being of all mankind. This approach continued through the festivals of 1949 (Budapest) and 1951 (East Germany), in line with Soviet policy, which was then emphasizing the division of the world into two antagonistic camps.

The festival in East Berlin in 1951, at the height of the Korean war, saluted the conversion of China to a Communist state in October 1949 and condemned the United Nations action in Korea. The North Korean "youth" delegation included many uniformed officers who had fought against American "imperialist aggressors," and who were feted as "heroes in the struggle for peace." The objective of the festival was to impress upon the participants that Communism represented peace, and to persuade the world at large that youth supported Communist objectives. International friendship themes were cleverly mixed with anti-American propaganda. The peace dove was made to symbolize the U.S.S.R. and was contrasted with the United States bird of war. The highpoint of the festival was a Peace March lasting many hours that featured anti-Western slogans and vigorous opposition to the efforts then under way for the creation of a West German military force. The role youth was expected to play in Communist attempts to disrupt these efforts, as well as the clearly partisan nature of the festival, was made clear in the speech by Walter Ulbricht, the leader of the East German Socialist Unity Party (Communist) on the occasion of the Peace March. West German "peace fighters" were called upon to resist the remilitarization of West Germany by:

1. Publicizing the threat to Germany posed by the presence of U. S. and U. K. "interventionist" troops in West Germany.
2. Intensifying demands for a plebiscite against remilitarization and for a peace treaty.
3. Having youth put up solid national resistance to West German "war preparations."
4. Defying the ban imposed by the West German government on the Communist youth organization, the *Freie Deutsche Jugend* (FDJ).
5. Breaking up the coalition policy of the Social Democrats in the trade unions as a "sell-out" to West German industrialists.
6. Developing the broadest possible protest movement against military conscription in West Germany.
7. Mobilizing all West German youth against the rebirth of the *Wehrmacht*.[2]

In discussing the "cultural" presentations of the various national delegations, a non-Communist observer of the festival has described, in a particularly revealing passage, the extent to which Communist propaganda at the height of Cold War antagonisms was based on appeals to raw and primitive emotions.

The most impressive part of the North Korean program...was a type of music-drama. At the outset, a North Korean mother appears on stage carrying a small bundle and bitterly spitting invectives into the air. The bundle, as I determined from the program notes to which I was frequently compelled to refer during the performance, represents her baby, who has just been killed in a "savage American bombing attack." Screaming a strident "Vengeance! Vengeance!" the woman places the deceased child on the stage and proceeds to execute a grotesque kind of dance. Her further screams, according to the program notes, are curses. After about ten minutes of her almost savage manifestation of hatred for Americans, the curtain falls on the first scene.

When the curtain opens on the next scene, the woman is seen creeping stealthily forward toward an American encampment near the battle lines. Both hands are clutching hand grenades which she is preparing to throw into the encampment. As she throws them, her screams echo, "Vengeance at last." Both grenades explode in the encampment, followed by groans of pain. Looking into the scene of carnage, the woman breaks into a horribly macabre dance of ecstasy. Her dance is soon interrupted by three "American soldiers," who dash out of the encampment and capture her. She hisses, spits, twists; but they manage to hold her.

As soon as the three "American soldiers" came out on the stage, the 1500 mixed delegates of the audience simultaneously and spontaneously rose to their feet in a paroxysm of passion, chanting: "Down with Truman! Down with Eisenhower! Down with MacArthur!" . . . . This demonstration against Americans lasted for close to ten minutes.

Enhancing the Communist representation of "American soldiers" were the "uniforms" that the actors wore. The pants were crumpled, the jackets extended to the knees. Key chains extended down to the ankles. The hats were rakishly cocked. The lieutenant wore a pair of pearl-handled six-guns in heavy ornate holsters. Cigarettes dangled from each mouth, and all three chewed gum violently.

As soon as the audience had settled back from its manifestation of scorn for the Americans, the play continued with the "American soldiers" inflicting their brutal assaults on the woman. Indeed, every adjective applied to Americans by Communist propagandists was brought to symbolic life by the actions of the young men playing the parts of American soldiers.

When the soldiers tire of punishing the woman, they decide to shoot her. At this point, however, an argument arises. Everyone wants the honor of doing the shooting. To settle the question, finally, the lieutenant produces a pair of dice and the three soldiers assume the proper position. The lieutenant laughs viciously when he wins the honor. Raising his gun with a cruel snarl, he aims carefully at the woman tied against a tree and prepares to pull the trigger.

Suddenly, out of the hills surrounding the encampment swarm the North Korean soldiers, just in time to rescue the woman. Again the sweating delegates rose in vigorous chant: "Kim Il Sung! Kim Il Sung!" He is the leader of the North Korean forces.

Within a few minutes the first chant faded into a far crisper and enthusiastic repetition of the names of "Stalin! Mao Tse-tung! Kim Il Sung!" The second chant continued for close to ten minutes, and then gave way to a rhythmic pounding of feet and hands to the tune of "The Song of Peace," "The Hymn to Stalin," "The Hymn to Mao Tse-tung . . . ."

The performers in the drama, at the start of the demonstration, came downstage and followed the audience in all their chants, songs, and cheers. Everyone in the theater had joined hands and was participating in the twenty minutes of madness.

In the excitement, the young flower girls at the foot of the stage, whose function it was to give flowers to each performer, began to throw their flowers up on the stage. The performers quickly picked up the flowers and threw them back. Thus, while the chants and songs throbbed mightily, a continuous barrage of flowers passed between the performers and the audience. It was the presence of mind of one of the stagehands, finally, that brought the curtain down quite abruptly and thereby curtailed the demonstration.

When the curtain again rose on the anti-climactic

finale, the woman was seen taking one of the pearl-handled revolvers from the American lieutenant and shooting him three times ... "Once for the honor of my murdered child ... once for my honor which you have sullied by force ... and once for the honor of our great Korean Motherland whose honor you will never sully."

Interestingly enough, the Korean woman had to use the pearl-handled revolver of the "American lieutenant" because the rescuing North Korean soldiers carried nothing more lethal than spears. This, obviously, was symbolic of their peaceful temperament.

As soon as the final curtain had fallen, the audience again took up the ardor of the previous demonstrations and continued it for close to fifteen minutes. As before, chants, songs, and cheers resounded mightily.[3]

This emotional, almost psychotic attitude toward Western countries and non-Communists in general continued to characterize the propaganda and meetings of the Communist front organizations until the death of Stalin. With the reorientation of Soviet policy that followed under Khrushchev, and signaled a departure from the barren aggressiveness of the Stalinist period, the Communist fronts adopted a much more sophisticated approach. In part, they may have learned something from one aspect of the festival in East Berlin that helped to offset the hypnotic effect produced by the mass and highly emotional demonstrations. The governments of West Germany and West Berlin had organized displays, lectures, concerts, movies, and other events, and made available much reading matter, to all of which the festival participants had access by crossing into West Berlin. This was important both for the large numbers of East German youths who were brought to East Berlin and for the foreign participants who were able to visit both halves of Berlin and compare for themselves.

Beginning in 1953, the youth festivals reflected the shift away from the hard line to a policy of "cooperation" and sought to garner prestige by presenting an appearance of reasonableness and backing a policy of "peaceful coexistence." Unity and cooperation of all the world's youth again became leading slogans. Yet, on the outside, this shift in tactics was seen precisely for what it was— a Communist tactic to recover lost influence and to gain lost ground. The new tactics did in some measure contribute to the effectiveness of the festivals, especially as the WFDY and the IUS were beginning to place emphasis on the underdeveloped countries, where an awareness of the political background of the festivals was not as great as it was among youth in Western countries.

The slogans of the Bucharest Festival—"Friendship forever!" "Gathering youth of all views to voice their desire to avert war" and "Long live peace!"—reflected this change in tactics.[4] The festival issued an appeal calling on youth everywhere to unite so that: "Negotiations will succeed in place of force ... each country will be master of its own affairs, and relations, based on confidence and equal status, will be established between the nations, and cultural and sports exchanges will be developed, thereby leading to better understanding among young people."[5] Youth was thus to be used as a lever to generate pressure to further East-West negotiations and to encourage a public mood favoring "settlement at any price."

Meeting in Warsaw after the Summit Conference in Geneva in July 1955, the Fifth World Youth Festival again emphasized "peace and friendship." "Let us reinforce again the activities that are more necessary than ever to assure peace. Let us work together for the relaxation of international tension, for disarmament, for the prohibition of atomic weapons and all means of mass destruction."[6] Yet, even so, the Communists used the festival as an arena for their efforts at moral polarization depicting the U.S.S.R. as being for peace, friendship, and the welfare of all humanity and the U. S. as the source of all evils besetting the world. Marching under a banner reading "No more Hiroshimas," the Japanese delegation helped to associate the U. S. with the dangers—real and imaginary—of atomic weapons. Sober representation of complex problems was never allowed to interfere with the Communist caricature in black and white. Conforming with Soviet policy, which sought. to put pressure on the United States and its European allies to reduce nuclear armaments and prohibit their use, so as to weaken Western military strength in the face of preponderant Soviet conventional armaments, the festival appeal stressed the banning of the atomic bomb, an approach calculated to impress honest and idealistic non-Communist young people, especially in Asia and Africa, who were emotionally overwhelmed by the existence of nuclear weapons.

The Sixth Festival was the first to be held inside the Soviet Union, in Moscow during August 1957. Conditions were far from auspicious from the Soviet viewpoint. The denunciation of Stalin in Khrushchev's secret Twentieth Party Congress speech in February 1956, the relaxation of controls that followed, and the widespread repercussions both outside and within the Soviet bloc after the events in Poland and the Hungarian revolution all served to create much intellectual and emotional ferment. The presence of youth from many countries could not help but make the imposition of an "official" line more difficult for the Communist sponsors. The Hungarian revolt received the greatest amount of attention—albeit not officially— in the many meetings and discussions that filled the festival. It was also the subject of much debate between festival delegates and ordinary Soviet citizens. The impact of such exchanges on those involved is difficult to evaluate. During official meetings, Soviet youth representatives were able to control the course of discussion fairly well. In the spontaneous meetings and discussions outside the festival program, however, no such control could be effectively exercised. Hence the introduction into the festival of anti-Soviet views on the Hungarian uprising almost certainly led to a good deal of "soul-searching" on the part of many participants, both Communist and otherwise.

The over-all effect of the festival on Soviet youth became a subject of considerable concern to the Soviet authorities. Preparations for the festival had begun long before it was to take place. Soviet youth publications had devoted a great deal of attention to the planned activities. Much had been done to cultivate a belief among Soviet students that the Communist sympathizers attending the festival were actually representative of the youth of their respective countries. The Soviet youth press warned immediately after the festival against harmful "bourgeois influences" allegedly introduced by alien elements of the festival,[7] apparently because the impression made by non-Communist, or at least non-Soviet, delegates was stronger than the authorities had anticipated.

PROBLEMS OF ORGANIZATION AND CONTROL

Besides being an occasion for demonstrating in support of Soviet programs and policies, the World Youth Festivals are an interesting study in mass political organization and control. Despite the fact that many non-Communist youths have attended the festivals, particularly the last two, which were held in Vienna and Helsinki, the Communist sponsors have been able to exercise fairly strict control over the proceedings. Several devices have been used to assure this control. While the festivals are sponsored by the WFDY and IUS, actual preparations are made behind the façade of an "international preparatory committee" (IPC), the officers of which have always included a large number of longtime WFDY-IUS functionaries. Through the Warsaw Festival in 1953, the IPCs were composed primarily of the WFDY and IUS personnel, but those for the Moscow (1957), Vienna (1959), and Helsinki (1962) festivals were broadened to include numerous non-Communists, even though the WFDY and IUS representatives retained control.[8] The coopted non-Communists were evidently carefully selected for their sympathetic attitudes, while the Soviet youth organization for its part has never relinquished its dominant planning function.

The sponsors' role in the preparations has been increasingly played down as their Communist character has become more widely appreciated. The IPCs therefore operate through a series of national festival committees that are, in turn, controlled by local supporters of the WFDY and the IUS, but also include other individuals not associated with any recognized Communist organization. These national festival committees pose as non-partisan bodies even though they have always been most unrepresentative of the national youth movement. The national representatives in the IPC are therefore in almost all cases members of one or more small, distinctly un-representative, national Communist or Communist front organizations, and as the national festival committees select the "official" national delegations to the festivals, this results in the selection of delegates who, if not under direct Communist control, are at any rate sufficiently pliable for Communist purposes.

Although participation by non-Communists is certainly welcomed and encouraged, control of the proceedings is assured through the selection of "representative" speakers at official functions. The U. S., British, and French delegations to the Moscow Festival in 1957, for example, contained a variety of youth groups, ranging from impressionable teenagers to clearly leftist youths of both the moderate and extreme varieties. There were also some anti-Soviet youths and those who represented a basically non-partisan viewpoint. The official national delegates in seminars, meetings, and official functions were, however, in almost all cases, members of the small and unrepresent-ative extreme left who had been selected by the Communist-controlled national festival committees.

Another means of controlling the proceedings is through the financial assistance provided by Communist governments. The IPCs have claimed that youth throughout the world financed the preparatory work and traveling and living expenses of the delegates. An International Solidarity Fund, to which the national Communist and Communist-front organizations contribute, was established to support those delegates who could not afford to pay their own way—especially those from Asia, Africa, and Latin America. According to a report in the Soviet *Komsomolskaya Pravda* a month before the Moscow Festival, the International Fund had collected $ 213,000,[9] but it is difficult to see how this would go very far in supporting even a fraction of the approximately 18,000 participants, much less provide for all the necessary services. The same report said that of the $ 552,000 required for the expenses of Latin American delegates, only 10 per cent would come from the Fund. Where the far from affluent Latin American Communists were to find the remainder was not mentioned, which suggests that there probably was massive but hidden help from the Soviet government.

Even some of the U. S. delegates traveled by air from San Francisco to Moscow and back for $ 300, when the normal tourist fare at that time was over $ 1000, and similar transportation assistance was offered elsewhere as well. The participants lived in a "Festival City" especially constructed in Moscow for the occasion. Buses, free medical aid, barber and beautician services, laundry, cleaning, and shoe repair were given free of charge. The Soviet government also provided logistical support for the work of the IPC, which was located in Moscow.

An estimate of $ 100,000,000 has been made for the cost to the Soviet government of the 1957 festival.[10] This was in good part defrayed by a lottery run by the Committee of Youth Organizations of the U.S.S.R. (KMOSSSR) in the amount of 600,000,000 rubles.[11] For handling the financial arrangements for the Vienna Festival in 1959 an enterprise was founded in Austria jointly by the IPC, an Austrian travel agent, and a firm that had financed the World Peace Council before its expulsion from Austria in 1957. But while money was raised through the sale of festival buttons, flags, and other fund raising devices, as well as through the resources of the International Solidarity Fund, most of the funds again evidently came from direct appropriations by Communist governments.

THE IMPORTANCE OF INDOCTRINATION

The propaganda circulated by the IPCs in preparing for the youth festivals has claimed that the festivals are non-political and not to be used for "party purposes." in fact, however, the festivals have been not only political, but partisan. In Communist jargon, the festivals "contribute to the consolidation of the democratic forces of youth in capitalist and dependent colonial countries."[12] The Communists have made a concerted attempt to influence the most likely prospects among nationalist youth of the underdeveloped countries by assisting them to attend festivals, and taking them on "grand tours" of the Communist countries afterwards. Since 1953 the political indoctrination aspects of the festivals have been played down in favor of mass psychological appeals such as cultural and sports events and large-scale demonstrations. Serious questions have been glossed over, while attempts have been made to win acceptance for emotional slogans.

In recent years the Communists have clearly sought to attract as large and as diverse a following as possible. The IPCs have stated on many occasions that the festivals are "open to all young people, irrespective of convictions, race, religious creed, and nationality. No political, philosophical, or religious trends will prevail ...."[13] The Communist-controlled IPC, however, is always the judge of what constitutes the aspirations and interests of the youth, and what actions can best further its aims. The efforts of the Communist organizers to impart a non-partisan character to the festivals include the solicitation of expressions of approval of the theme and aims of festivals from prominent national personalities and efforts to have such people become members of national festival committees. The last few festivals have emphasized cultural and sports events and, in the words of the then President of the WFDY, Bruno Bernini, "... the organization of special demonstrations [allowing] us to draw in a larger number of young people and cultural organizations."[14]

The festivals are so organized that there will be something for everyone to do at all times. The intensity of activity is such as to overwhelm many participants with a feeling of being in the midst of a world-shaking event. A typical festival program is packed with scheduled activities. An opening ceremony gets the program under way. A big parade, with flags and banners, seeks to generate a mood of unity behind a set of pre-determined slogans. At Moscow in 1957, however, the political overtones were introduced early when, at the opening ceremony, the President of the Supreme Soviet, Chief of State Voroshilov, equated the Soviet system with peace and the future of mankind:

> We have never imposed, nor are we going to impose, our ideas and our views upon anyone. And if the great ideas of Socialism triumph in the course of historic development and ever more countries and peoples are taking the road of Socialist development, this of course is not a matter of propaganda, it is law governing the historical development of society, for Socialism is the most progressive social system, most suited to satisfy the needs and aspirations of the peoples.[15]

The program is usually oriented around a number of discussions, meetings, and demonstrations at which the themes of the festival are discussed in conjunction with social activities and numerous cultural events. In these sessions the speakers, carefully chosen, elaborate on the particular political or ideological line. A young Latin American Communist or sympathizer, for example, will discuss the conditions in his country or area, denouncing "imperialist" intervention and exploitation with more or less oblique references to the adverse effects of U. S. policy. Conditions are portrayed factually enough but in a one-sided manner, which gives no account of progress made and being made. The causes are portrayed in black and white, with the "forces of progress" arrayed against those of the "exploiters."

A number of big demonstrations usually rally support for specific themes such as anti-A-bomb testing, anti-German rearmament, anti-colonialism. At Moscow there was a large Youth Meeting for Peace and Friendship, which took place on the anniversary of the bombing of Hiroshima. Pictorial displays and movies were used to show the horrors of the attack.

An overwhelming number of social and cultural events fills out the festival program. Sports play a big role. The Soviet Union and the other Communist countries usually see to it that many of their top international and Olympic athletes are present for the competition. A Students' Carnival, a "Grand Carnival of Youth," and a Kremlin Ball were some of the social highlights at the Moscow Festival.

After the festival ends, what is perhaps the most significant aspect of the festival activities begins. Large numbers of selected participants are taken on tours of the Soviet Union and other Communist countries. These carefully guided tours are calculated to impress youths, especially from developing countries, with the achievements of the Soviet system.

All this notwithstanding, at Vienna in 1959 the Communists experienced serious difficulties in conducting a controlled mass rally in the face of organized "counter-propaganda" efforts by non-Communist youth. For the first time there was no monopoly over the information available to the festival participants. For the first time also there was no governmental support for the festival organizers.[16]

Not only did the Eighth World Youth Festival in Helsinki in the summer of 1962 have to operate under these disadvantageous conditions, but the budget for the festival had been drastically reduced.[17] This alone contributed in part to the disenchantment of many of the participants, since living conditions and travel and other facilities were not so comfortable as at past festivals. Such disenchantment was particularly evident among Asian and African groups. For instance, a lack of funds led to the housing of all English-speaking African students together, which was not astute given the acute African sensibilities to segregationist practices. Nor was it particularly effective to assault neutralists with a long agenda of partisan events. All forty-six of the non-Communist participants from Ceylon left the festival. Nigerian, Ugandan, and Indonesian participants publicly expressed their resentment, and many others did so privately.

In the beginning, the festivals were one of the few opportunities for bringing large numbers of African, Asian, and Latin American young people to the Eastern European countries. Today, with large numbers of students in the Soviet Union and the other Eastern European countries, and with Soviet and Eastern European embassies and trade missions in most of the under-developed countries, this motive for the festivals is no longer compelling. Neither is the use of festivals to provide youth within the Communist countries with an illusion of contact with the outside world. As a result of the significant expansion of foreign tourism, the presence of many Western students in the Soviet Union, the large number of cultural and sports exchanges, and the increasing though still limited opportunities of Communist youth for travel, the festivals are becoming an increasingly superfluous means of fulfilling this objective.

The replacement of anti-Western colonialism by neutralist nationalism in the newly free countries in Africa, together with the taking over of the local Communist youth and student fronts by many of the new nationalist and one-party regimes, has deprived the Communists of much of their former initiative on matters of anti-colonialism, which they actively exploited at the festivals. These new developments have also made it impossible for local Communists or sympathizers to determine the selection of African students to attend the festivals.

The ninth World Youth Festival was to be held in the summer of 1965 in Algeria. Considerable doubt existed for some time as to whether the Communists would hold another festival. The WFDY Executive Committee session in July 1964 decided to go ahead with another festival,

despite the marginal utility of the eighth festival in Helsinki. An International Preparatory Committee was
formed in September 1964, but efforts to prepare for the
festival were in abeyance until a decision was made by
WFDY and IUS leaders as to the location. With the
decision to hold the festival in Algiers, the IPC Secretariat opened there in November 1964. The official host
is the Algerian National Preparatory Committee, headed
by President Ben Bella and other notables of the
Algerian regime. In addition to the usual sports, cultural
and other events and meetings, the IPC has decided to
emphasize meetings of solidarity with the peoples fighting
in the Congo, Angola, South Vietnam, South Africa and
elsewhere "for freedom."

The organizers of the festivals hope that by holding
the festival in Africa, under the patronage of the Algerian
regime, large participation from African countries will be
assured. The control of the festival and its proceedings
remains in the hands of the WFDY and the IUS, despite
efforts or expectations by the Algerians themselves to
maintain control. The effect that this will have on festival
participation and proceedings remains to be seen.

If the world conference of Communist parties planned
for 1965 should result in a clear split between the Soviet
and Chinese Communist parties, the 1965 World Youth
Festival could provide an opportunity for the pro-Soviet
forces to demonstrate in support of their position. The
IUS-WFDY leaders would probably take those steps necessary to make certain that pro-Chinese elements would have
no opportunity to turn the Festival into a demonstration
of Sino-Soviet name-calling and mutual invective. Should
the Sino-Soviet controversy remain papered-over as at
present by the avoidance of a formal split, it will be
interesting to see how the WFDY and IUS leaders handle
the pro-Chinese elements. It is quite conceivable that
both pro-Soviet and pro-Chinese elements will avoid
recriminations should the situation in Vietnam remain
threatening. In such an event, the propaganda gains to
the Communists could be considerable.

6/Chapter
The Youth Movements in the Communist Countries (1945 — 1964)

After World War II the Soviet Communist Party took steps to turn the Komsomol back from military and defense support activities to the tasks that had been set for youth in the late 1930s: the building of a mass organization through relaxed membership requirements in order to facilitate the political and ideological indoctrination of the large mass of Soviet youth. Communist ideological control had been severely disrupted during the war. Widespread disaffection, unrest caused by opportunities for young Soviet soldiers to observe life in the West, and the disappointment of many at the regime's failure to relax its dictatorial controls made the re-imposition of that control after the war all the more necessary. An evident lack of interest in ideological matters on the part of young people who had gone through the rigors and privations of a terrible war led to a sharp drop in Komsomol membership, from a wartime peak of about 15 million to about 8 or 9 million in 1948. Youth was apathetic toward political affairs, and much more interested in improving the severely reduced material conditions of life. Frequent recruitment drives from 1949 on have raised the membership, to about 20 million (January 1963),[1] but the apathy remains.

THE SOVIET KOMSOMOL

The essential nature of the Komsomol in the postwar period has remained unchanged from the early days. The role of the youth organization in Soviet society, and its relation to the Communist Party as set forth in the Party Statutes, have remained virtually the same for over forty years. The section of the Party Statutes, as approved by the Twenty-second Party Congress in October 1961. dealing with the Komsomol is as follows:

VII. The Party and the Young Communist League

60.   The All-Union Leninist Young Communist League [Komsomol] is an organization of young people, and active assistant and reserve of the Party. The Young Communist League helps the Party to rear young people in the spirit of Communism, to enlist them in the practical work of building a new society, and to train a generation of harmoniously developed people who will live, work, and direct public affairs under Communism.

61.   The YCL works under the guidance of the Communist Party of the Soviet Union. The work of the local YCL organizations is directed and supervised by the appropriate republic, territory, province, region, city, and district Party organizations.

In their work in the Communist education of young people, local Party bodies and primary Party organizations rely on Young Communist League organizations and support and disseminate their useful undertakings.

63.   YCL members who are admitted to the Party leave the Young Communist League from the moment they join the Party, unless they occupy

executive posts in Young Communist League
organizations.[2]

As stated at this Congress by Nikita Khrushchev, the
Komsomol is one of the mass organizations of the working
people, along with the soviets, the trade unions, the co-
operatives, and cultural and educational groups. These
organizations remain the "transmission belts," even if no
longer so identified, of the Stalinist period by which Party
directives are transmitted and applied to, and support for
Party policy created in, the population at large.

Apart from the intensive indoctrination efforts
imposed on the Komsomol, the practical tasks assigned to
the youth of the Soviet Union in the post-war period were
all associated with the enormous task of reconstruction and
development. Youth was called upon to take the lead in
fulfilling the first post-war Five-Year Plan. The task of raising the leveled Stalingrad (now Volgograd) to a modern
city became a special project of the Komsomol. Youth was
also called upon to play an important role in the "virgin
lands" program, by which new lands were to be opened
for cultivation so as to increase Soviet agricultural output.

The most recent Komsomol Congress (the Fourteenth), in April 1962, made it clear that the main task
of the Komsomol is to mobilize all youth, both Komsomol
members and non-members, in the campaign for increased
productivity and "creating the material and technical bases
of Communism."[3] The Komsomol Central Committee
took it upon itself, without consulting the membership
and clearly under a directive of the Party Central Committee, "to declare Komsomol patronage over the erection
of nineteen thermal, atomic, and hydroelectric power
stations, the electrification of 10,000 kilometers of railway,
and the construction of major transmission lines . . . . [and
to help] collective and state farms to mechanize 30,000
livestock sections by 1965 . . . ."[4] Increases in labor productivity through the introduction of "progressive production methods"; assistance in the construction of major
chemical plants and combines; the growing of big corn

crops, which "has become the most urgent cause of the rural Komsomol";[5] work in the virgin lands; more responsibilities for the training of labor reserves (vocational training); raising the general educational level of young workers; increased ideological work based on the new Party program adopted at the Twenty-second Congress in October 1961; "strengthening the ties between school and life more actively"; "strengthening friendship and cooperation with the youth of the world"; and improved organizational work were some of the tasks accepted by the Komsomol Congress.[6]

Komsomol aid to the World Federation of Democratic Youth and the International Union of Students was also emphasized at the Komsomol Congress, these organizations being characterized as having "won general recognition among the progressive youth of the world by their consistent fight for peace, national independence, democracy, and the rights of the young generation."[7] The presidents of the WFDY and the IUS both addressed the Congress, as did representatives from various other foreign Communist youth organizations. Only the Albanian youth organization was missing, and the Congress not surprisingly reflected the views of the Soviet party by attacking the Albanians, since they "aimed at weakening the solidarity of the youth movement of the socialist countries and causing a split in it."[8]

The structure of the Komsomol follows that of the Communist Party of the Soviet Union.[9] The highest governing body is in theory the Congress, which is supposed to be elected from lower bodies to meet once every four years. Since the death of Stalin, the Komsomol Congresses have met regularly in 1954, 1958, and 1962. Between 1936 and 1954, however, there was only one Congress (1949), as indeed between 1939 and 1952 there were no Party Congresses. In fact, the Congresses remain demonstrations at which the membership at large, through local functionaries, is rallied behind the policies of the leadership. The Congresses also serve to provide the participating functionaries with a measure of social standing, the honor of attending the Congress and a visit to Moscow serving as rewards for loyal service to the leadership.

The hierarchical organizational structure of the Komsomol has its roots in the primary organizations located wherever youth is active—factories, collective and state farms, the various levels of the school and university system, and the armed forces. The basic Komsomol units are led by a secretary, with the larger ones having what amounts to an executive committee as well as a secretary. Following the Party system, the Komsomol units are organized in the form of an ascending pyramid, with each body under the supervision of the next higher one. The primary organizations are guided by rural or town Komsomol committees, which in turn go up through the district, regional, and republican committees to the Central Committee at the top. At all levels above the primary organization a conference or Congress exists as the formal governing body, electing the committees and secretaries at each level.

The effective center of control in the Komsomol lies in its Central Committee, which is formally elected by the quadrennial All-Union Congress, but in practice is appointed by the Party Central Committee. The latest composition of the Central Committee included 145 members and 68 candidates.[10] Within this relatively large body, the effective decision-making power appears to lie in a Bureau that carries on the work of the Komsomol between Central Committee meetings (plenums). Supporting the work of the Central Committee and its Bureau is a large Secretariat. The First Secretary of the Komsomol exercises general direction over the work of the Central Committee, and thus over the Komsomol as a whole.[11] As with the Party, the practice whereby full-time secretaries at each level are designated by the next highest committee, then formally elected by the committee they serve, enables the secretaries at the top to install personnel of their own choosing, thus controlling all Komsomol activities.

The Komsomol has many responsibilities, the specific nature of which vary with Party policies. Of greatest importance perhaps is the use of the Komsomol as an instrument of political indoctrination to develop a new generation, loyal, eager, and prepared to assume the task of creating a Communist society.

Party activities among youth cover the entire range of the school age population. The age limits of the Komsomol itself are from fourteen to twenty-eight.[12] From ages six to nine children are organized in the "Little Octobrists." Formed in the mid-1920s to provide organized and politically oriented recreational and pre-school activities for the younger children, the "Little Octobrists" were abolished during World War II when the chaos caused by the military situation disrupted the program of pre-school education.[13] From ten to fifteen almost all young people are enrolled in the Young Pioneers. Highly organized and working under a Komsomol leader, the Pioneers are given heroic stories about Lenin and other Party leaders. The fairy tales, adventure stories, and heroic epics of non-Communist societies have their counterpart in the Communist indoctrinational programs. The difference is that all Pioneer and Komsomol activities are designed to inculcate in youth the currently accepted party ideology. The Komsomol has the main responsibility for this work among the Pioneers. It also has responsibility for carrying on an extensive program of political education for older youth outside the school system. This is done primarily through discussion circles, special schools, and particularly through the youth press, of which *Komsomolskaya Pravda* (Komsomol Truth) and *Molodoi Kommunist* (Young Communist) are the cornerstones. In addition, in 1962, the Komsomol published about two hundred other newspapers and magazines.

The Soviet Union is represented in the World Federation of Democratic Youth by the Committee of Youth Organizations of the U.S.S.R. (KMOSSSR), which was set up officially in July 1956. Its forerunner was the Anti-Fascist Committee of Soviet Youth formed in September 1941 to conduct anti-fascist and pro-Soviet propaganda among the young people of the world during the war, as well as to be the focus of the wartime "anti-fascist" fronts among the youth.[14]

> The purpose of the Committee of Youth Organizations of the U.S.S.R. is to coordinate the activities of member organizations on questions of common interests; to facilitate in every way the further strengthening of the friendship and cooperation between Soviet young people and those of other countries, and the extension of the organizational ties of Soviet young people with international and national youth student organizations, movements, and groups; to contribute to the development of an international outlook on the part of Soviet young people and to mobilize them for the fight for peace and friendship.[15]

The membership of KMOSSSR includes the Komsomol and Pioneer organizations, various sports societies, the youth sections of various trade unions, the youth sections of the Union of Red Cross and Red Crescent societies, the All-Russian Society for the Preservation of Nature, and others.[16] There are, in addition, under KMOSSSR two formally autonomous bodies that are active in international activities—the Student Council of the U.S.S.R., which represents the U.S.S.R. in the International Union of Students, and the Bureau of International Youth Tourism, "Sputnik."[17]

Formally an autonomous body coordinating "the activities of Soviet youth organizations, primarily in matters of cooperation with foreign youth organizations,"[18] KMOSSSR is actually a department of the Central Committee of the Komsomol for work with non-Communist foreign youth organizations.

One of the most important results of the Second World War was the extension of Soviet power into Eastern Europe, China, Korea, and Vietnam.

Wherever the Communists have succeeded in assuming power one of their first actions has been to organize youth. In the immediate post-war years, the new Communist-dominated governments in Eastern Europe followed closely the Soviet pattern for organizing youth. However, the path to the creation of a large, monopolistic youth organization on the Soviet model was traveled in stages. Although complete Communist domination of the political life of Eastern Europe had been achieved by the end of 1948, in some countries the formation of centralized, Party-controlled youth organizations took somewhat longer.

The degree to which the various Communist regimes have been successful in winning support from youth has varied. Since the "thaw" following Stalin's death, and especially since Khrushchev's "secret speech" to the Twentieth Congress of the Soviet party in February 1956 and the events in Poland and Hungary later that year, youth in Eastern Europe has been particularly restless and hostile to the Communist regimes.

The age limits for Communist youth organizations outside the U.S.S.R. seem to have been standardized at fourteen to twenty-six. All the youth organizations also sponsor and direct children's organizations on the "Little Octobrist" and Young Pioneers model. In Hungary, China, North Korea, and North Vietnam a council or committee similar to the Soviet KMOSSSR has been formed to integrate all youth and student activities. One significant difference between the U.S.S.R. and the other Communist countries is that in some cases, such as Hungary, Poland, Yugoslavia, and the Asian countries, the regimes have had to forego their desire to incorporate the students as a section of the larger youth organizations.

POLAND

Until 1948 there were in Poland four major youth movements, each associated with one of the major political parties.[19] The largest was the young peasants' movement, numbering 500,000 in 1947, but this was divided into supporters of the large representative People's Peasant Party under Mikolajczyk and a Communist puppet peasant party. The Communist youth organization (200,000 in 1946) had been formed in the early 1920s, but had soon been declared illegal and remained so until after the war. The Union of Youth for Struggle (ZWM) was organized at the war's end as an auxiliary of the Communist Polish Worker' Party. A good-sized Socialist youth organization attached to the pre-war Polish Socialist Party also existed (120,000 in 1947), but it was gradually infiltrated by Communists who purged the non-Communists from positions of leadership. By March 1948 it had become for all purposes a puppet organization, and took steps to leave the Socialist youth international (International Union of Socialist Youth). A small liberal-democratic youth organization representing some intellectual and middle-class youth also existed (20,000 in 1946).

By early 1948, after Mikolajczyk's flight to the West and the destruction of the Peasant Party, the Communists were able to demand and obtain a fusion of the central committees of the four organizations and the formation of a united central committee. Shortly thereafter, in July 1948, a "unity" congress took place at which the four youth organizations merged into the *Zwiazek Mlodziezy Polskiej* —ZMP (Union of Polish Youth). Membership grew from 413,000 in July 1948 to 2,018,000 in February 1955 as the new Communist regime put strong pressure on youth to join.

A similar fate befell the four student organizations that existed after the war, again set up on political lines associated with the major parties. A separate student organization, *Zwiazek Akademickiej Mlodziezy Polskiej* —ZAMP (Polish Academic Youth Union), was created by merger of these groups at the same time that the youth organizations were unified. In August 1950 the ZMP and the ZAMP were ordered to merge by the end of the year, in line with the Soviet practice of gathering all young people into one organization.

CZECHOSLOVAKIA

In Czechoslovakia the first Communist youth organization was formed in 1921, shortly after the formation of the Republic, when the Communists succeeded in capturing the Socialist youth organizations in Slovakia and the German-speaking areas, splitting the Czech Socialist youth, and fusing all three groups into the rudiments of a national Communist youth organization. After exercising considerable influence during its first few years of existence, the Communist youth organization continued to function legally, but under government-imposed restrictions, and as a distinct minority group. The banning of the Communists in Czechoslovakia after the Munich Agreement of 1938 and before the German occupation of all of Czechoslovakia in March 1939 ended its legal activities altogether. Until May 1945 the Communist youth organizations worked under the Communist Party as part of the national resistance movement.

In June 1945 the national Socialists, the Social Democrats, and the Communists agreed to create a "national bloc" of Socialist parties inside the National Front. They also decided to create an inter-party Czechoslovak Youth Union (*Ĉeskoslovanský Svaz Mládeze*—CSM) in which the Communist youth organization was only one constituent part. In February 1948, at the time of the Communist coup, the CSM was taken over completely by the Communists, and in April 1949 it was transformed into a national youth organization.[20] Not until June 1958, however, was the CSM formally affiliated with the Czechoslovak Communist Party.

One concession to nationalism was the creation under the national Central Committee of a Slovak Central Committee of the CSM in Bratislava.

The CSM forms part of the Communist-dominated National Front, which unites all political and social organizations under the leadership of the Communist Party. The Slovakian Central Committee of the CSM forms part of the National Front in Slovakia.

The Czechoslovak Pioneers were formed in 1949. The publications of the CSM include *Mladá Fronta*, *Mladý Svet*, and *Smena* (Slovak).

HUNGARY

All of the political parties in Hungary had youth organizations after the war, the best organized of which was the Communist,[21] while the others were also infiltrated by them. An ostensibly non-party body, the Hungarian Democratic Youth Federation, loosely linked these organizations. It was not long, however, before the various youth organizations began to merge. In the summer of 1946 the religious youth organizations were dissolved by the Communist-dominated Hungarian government under pressure from the Soviet chairman of the Allied Control Commission. By the end of 1947 all non-Communist youth organizations had been disbanded, and the Hungarian Democratic Youth Federation replaced by the People's Federation of Hungarian Youth. This latter body served to coordinate and guide the activities of the Communist youth organizations. In February 1950, by which time all left-wing Socialists and other non-Communists had been purged from leading positions, all of these youth organizations were united into the *Dolgozo Ifjusag Szövetsége*—DISZ (Federation of Working Youth); and in 1951 the Communists formally incorporated the DISZ into the party as its youth organization.

YUGOSLAVIA

In Yugoslavia, as World War II was drawing to a close, Tito formed a People's Front out of the wartime National Liberation Front, which united representatives of various parties under the firm control of the Communist Party. Shortly after the war, steps were taken to reorganize the United Union of Anti-Fascist Youth of Yugoslavia, which had been set up under Communist control during the war.[22] The name was changed to *Narodna Omladina Yugoslavia*—PYY (People's Youth of Yugoslavia) at a congress in Zagreb in May 1946. Alongside this front there also existed the Union of Communist Youth of Yugoslavia,

Savez Kommunistichki Omladine Yugoslavia, which had been formed in 1919 and had worked illegally and underground from then up to the liberation of the country from the Germans in 1944. In 1949 the two were merged to form one Party organization modeled after the Soviet Komsomol, retaining the name of People's Youth of Yugoslavia. The name was changed to *Savez Omladine Yugoslavia*—UYY (Union of Youth of Yugoslavia) in January 1963. The problems of nationalism in Yugoslavia are handled, as far as the youth organization is concerned, by allowing each national republic to have its own youth organizational structure from primary organization to Congress and Central Committee. The national Congress and Central Committee provide unified direction and guidance under Party control. The periodical of the UYY is *Mladost* (Youth).

ROMANIA

In Romania a Communist youth organization had existed from the early 1920s, but shortly after the end of World War II it was dissolved because it was not attracting any significant support.[23] Attempts to set up a broader organization to include all youth soon foundered, however, as the Communists lost control of it. Later, a Union of Working Youth (*Uniunea Tinerilov Muncitori*—UTM) was formed. Alongside this organization were special groups for young farmers, school children, young ethnic Hungarians in Transylvania, and a university students' organization (which had had its own independent process of development). In December 1948 the Central Committee of the Romanian Workers' Party decided to unify these various youth organizations, which was accomplished at a congress in March 1949. In early 1950 the students were given their own unions outside the UTM. The publications include *Scîuteia Tineretului* (Spark of the Youth) and *Tînărul Leninist* (The Young Leninist).

BULGARIA

The Bulgarian Communist youth organization has a long tradition going back to World War I. In the early post-World War I years it became the leading youth organization within the Bulgarian labor movement, but it was broken up and outlawed along with the Bulgarian Communist Party after an unsuccessful attempt to overthrow the government in 1923.

Soon after World War II the Communists, in power after the occupation of the country by Soviet military forces, attempted to unify all the existing youth organizations, but this proved to be somewhat premature.[24] During the war, in 1942, an underground coalition had been formed on the initiative of the Communists in order to oppose the Bulgarian government, then an Axis ally. Represented in this "Fatherland Front" were the Communists, the Radical Agrarians, Social Democrats, liberals, and authoritarian nationalists of the right. Although they had taken the lead in forming this underground coalition, the Communists remained in the background. Each of the parties represented in the coalition had a youth organization of its own, and when the Communists sought to unify all these youth groups in 1945, the other parties in the "Fatherland Front" opposed them.

However, by December 1947 the Communists had strengthened their position sufficiently so that the desired unification could take place. The Union of People's Youth was formed in December 1947 (in 1949 renamed Dimitrov Union of People's Youth, *Dimitrovski Suiuz na Narodnata Mladezh*—DSNM; then in 1958 given its present name of Dimitrov Communist Youth Union, *Dimitrovski Kommunisticheski Mladezhki Suivz*—DKMS, in both cases after the long-time Bulgarian Communist leader Georgi Dimitrov). The membership grew from 500,000 in 1947 to 900,000 in 1952, then to about 2 million in 1957 (including 700,000 Pioneers age nine to fourteen). The Bulgarian Communist youth organization is the only one to be organized on paramilitary lines. The members are trained to assist the militia and the frontier police. Its publications include *Narodna Mladezh* (People's Youth) and *Mladezh* (Youth).

ALBANIA

The Communist youth organization in Albania was formed in November 1941 as a section of the Communist Party.[25] During the war the party was also active in forming Anti-Fascist People's Youth Committees in the villages and towns and partisan groups in order to mobilize the youth against the Italians and Germans. A Union of Anti-Fascist Youth of Albania (BRASH) was formed from these committees at a congress in August 1944. The president and the secretary-general were members of the Communist youth organization. At its third congress in 1946 the name was changed to People's Youth of Albania. By resolution of the Albanian Communist Party in June 1949, the People's Youth of Albania and the other Communist youth organizations were ordered to merge. This was carried out at a congress in September 1949, where the Union of Working Youth of Albania (STMA) was founded.

CHINA

The youth of China, especially the students, has played an important role in the political life of the country ever since the founding of the Chinese Republic by Sun Yat-sen in 1911.[26] The Communists were particularly active in the years after World War I. One line of development was initiated by the new Russian Communist youth organization in 1918, and by 1920 a Socialist youth organization had also been formed out of the Left Socialist and anarcho-syndicalist elements of the left-wing student movement.[27] In 1921 it became more akin to a Communist organization with the expulsion of the syndicalists and the imposition of stronger discipline and centralization. Another line was the formation of a Communist youth group in Paris in the early 1920s by Chou En-lai and other young Chinese students and workers. On the whole, however, the Communist youth groups set up in China in the 1920s fared rather badly as a result of their suppression, first by Chiang Kaishek and then by the Japanese occupation authorities.

In the mid-thirties, Chinese Communist youth followed the Comintern-Chinese Communist Party decision to form front organizations with nationalist groups. Forming "popular youth organizations" under a more moderate platform and cooperation in the expulsion of the Japanese were to be the means to increase Communist influence. Two such "front" groups formed the basis for the Communist youth organization (New Democratic Youth League) set up by the Chinese Communist Party in January 1949. NDYL membership soared from 190,000 in April 1949 to 9 million in June 1953 as the Communists tightened their grip on the country. Two new front organizations, for work among the masses of politically unsophisticated youth, were also formed to function under NDYL direction, the All-China Federation of Students (March 1949) and All-China Federation of Democratic Youth (May 1949). These groups represent Communist China in the International Union of Students and the World Federation of Democratic Youth.

After the Chinese invasion of Tibet in 1951, the familiar process of "assimilation" took place there. The existing youth groups were put under Chinese leadership and made subject to control by the Chinese Communist Party. It was not until May 1963, however, that a Communist youth organization in the "Tibet Autonomous Region" of China could be formed and its first Congress held.[28] Apart from political difficulties, the long period necessary to organize a youth organization was in part due to the absence of a tradition of youth organizations in Tibet. The Chinese youth organization publishes a daily paper, *Chung-Kuo Ch'ing-nien* (China Youth).

NORTH KOREA AND NORTH VIETNAM

Relatively little information is available on the youth and student movements in the two Asian Communist countries of North Korea and North Vietnam. In both cases, however, the traditional Communist pattern has been followed.

The Korean Democratic Union of Youth was formed in January 1946 as a result of the merger of several youth groups already in existence. It is closely tied to the Korean Workers' Party (Communist). By 1950 its membership had reached 1,300,000. On January 17, 1951, the "democratic" youth unions in North and South Korea united into the Korean Democratic Union of Youth, which functions only in the North but claims to represent "the real interests" of all Korean youth.[29] The KDUY represents North Korea in the World Federation of Democratic Youth.

A succession of several Communist youth groups was formed by the Communists of Indo-China during the nineteen twenties and thirties. During World War II these groups were active in the underground resistance to the Japanese occupation. The Union of Youth of Vietnam was formed by the Ho Chi Minh Communists as a youth front organization at a congress in Hanoi in June 1946, and in February 1950 was transformed into the Federation of Vietnamese Youth (FVV), in which all youth organizations in northern Vietnam were included. At present the FVV, which is part of the Fatherland Front embracing all political and social organizations in North Vietnam, includes the Union of Working Youth of Vietnam (founded in 1956), the Vietnamese Student Union, the Vietnamese Pupil's Union, and various sports societies. It represents North Vietnam in the WFDY.

The Union of Working Youth of Vietnam is the equivalent of the Soviet Komsomol. Its relation to the Communist Party was spelled out at its Congress in 1961, when it was stated that "ever since its foundation the UWYV has always enjoyed the constant solicitude of the Vietnamese Workers' Party (Communist) and President Ho Chi Minh. The Union has been, and will always remain, the right arm and the loyal reserve of the Party."[30]

EAST GERMANY

The Communist youth organization in East Germany forms something of a special case. Organizationally, it is typical of all the Communist youth groups of Eastern Europe, but the troubles that the East German regime has had with youth are particularly revealing of the incipient hostility that has always existed between young people's ambitions and the doctrinaire goals of Communism. Moreover, the fact that Germany has remained a divided country in the heart of Europe has consistently worked to point up the contrasting fates of youth under Communism and in free societies. It is for this reason that the history and experience of the Free German Youth (FDJ) deserves more than passing attention.

A Communist youth organization had, of course, existed in Germany from 1918 until after the rise of Hitler, when it was forced to go underground or into exile. Many of its functionaries fled to the Soviet Union, whence they returned in 1945 to assume leadership of youth affairs in the Soviet zone of occupation.

In the first months after World War II the Soviet occupation authorities in Germany set up youth committees in their occupation zone.[31] These committees were in part led by left-wing inmates of former Nazi concentration camps. By decree of July 31, 1945, all youth organizations in the Soviet zone were dissolved, including the Boy Scouts and church groups, and the formation of new ones was prohibited. "Anti-fascist" youth committees were to be set up in all cities and medium-sized towns, the members of which were to be the most active "anti-fascist" boys and girls.

To exercise jurisdiction over these committees, a hierarchy of higher committees was created—committees at the *Länder* and province level were to direct the local committees, and a Central Youth Council (CYC) was to oversee the intermediate levels of control. A separate committee under the Central Youth Council was set up for

Berlin. The leaders of the CYC were two members of the Communist Party of Germany (KPD), and a member of the Social Democratic Party (SPD), Edith Baumann, who later became a member of the Communist Party.

Although a large number of committees was formed, the total membership remained rather small and distinctly left wing in political composition. The Communist arrogation of words such as "democratic" and "anti-fascist" for their purposes was typical. They first set up an organizational framework and then took steps to woo or pressure youth into it.

The formation of the current youth organization in the Soviet zone of Germany, the *Freie Deutsche Jugend*— FDJ (Free German Youth), took place in early 1946. The Central Executive was headed by a Communist, and contained a Communist majority. Youth representatives of the non-Communist parties participated in the hope of being able to exercise some influence. A provisional all-German leadership was elected in April in Berlin, through which, by appealing for German unity, the FDJ had hopes of extending its political influence outside the Soviet zone.

In June 1946 the first Congress (*Parlament*) of the FDJ was convened in Berlin with delegates from all the occupation zones, as well as an observer from the newly formed World Federation of Democratic Youth. The first *Parlament* was concerned above all with presenting the FDJ as an "above-party," all-German organization.[32] The term *Parlament* was chosen to describe the meeting in order to capitalize on the democratic connotations of the word. But the proceedings of the Congress showed the nature of the organization to be quite different.

The second *Parlament*, in May 1947, took steps to bind the members, including many non-Communists, closer to the Socialist Unity Party (Communist), and served as a rally in support of efforts to extend the Communist (KPD)-Socialist (SPD) party merger to all of Germany.[33]

The first inter-zonal discussions between the FDJ and the largest youth organizations in the Western occupation zones took place in Cologne in the latter part of 1947. Here the FDJ sought to win the support of their opposite numbers—the Catholic, Evangelical, Social Democratic, and *Bündische Jugend* youth organizations—for the creation of an all-German youth federation. The meeting, however, led only to a sharp controversy over political conditions in the Soviet zone, and the lack of freedom there for non-Communist youth groups. In January 1948 non-Communist youth rejected all cooperation with the FDJ in the Western zones. The FDJ was also unsuccessful in its effort to get trade unions in the Western zones to co-operate in youth affairs. The Soviet representatives pro-posed to the Allied Coordinating Committee in February 1948 that the FDJ be approved as a national organization, but this the Western powers rejected on the ground that no youth groups should be sanctioned on a national basis until German unification had been attained.

By early 1947 the FDJ had been established as the only youth organization in the Soviet zone. In the Western zones there were many youth organizations, the FDJ among them. In Berlin the FDJ could not officially func-tion at all because of the inability of the four powers to agree on a policy toward youth. Unofficially, however, the FDJ flourished in the Soviet sector.

The situation in the former capital was somewhat dif-ferent from that in the occupation zones. In December 1945 the youth committees formed by the various political parties had called for a united youth organization for Berlin. The four political parties that were allowed to operate—Social Democrats (SPD), Communists (KPD), Christian Democrats (CDU), and Liberals (LDP)—agreed on a constitution for a unified organization, but the Allied *Kommandatura* barred its formation. The Soviet authorities were for licensing only the FDJ, while the Western powers were for approving other youth organiza-tions as well.

Despite the fact that the leadership continuously took pains to stress that the FDJ was an "above party" organi-

zation its real nature as a partisan political movement was
the source of growing controversy between its Communist-
controlled SED majority and the minority supporting
either the CDU or the LDP. The changing character of
the FDJ central executive is an illuminating example of
its increasingly partisan nature. The first Secretariat (June
1946 - May 1947) had eight Communists and seven non-
Communists (all of whom were by no means anti-Communist); the second Secretariat (May 1947 - spring 1949)
had nine Communists and six non-Communists; all six of
the Secretariat members elected in the spring of 1949 were
SED members and thus Communists.

The differences between the SED majority and the
minority came to a head in the fall of 1947, when the
FDJ Secretariat would not protest the arrest of a CDU
youth leader in the Soviet zone by the Soviet secret police
on trumped-up charges of espionage. The minority
remained in the FDJ for the time being in order to try
to help non-Communist youth in the Soviet zone, but
when a wave of arrests of CDU and LDP youth functionaries ensued, the CDU and LDP representatives left the
FDJ central executive in January 1948. The non-Communist minority had simply been used by the Communists
for the sake of respectability and to bolster the claim that
the FDJ was a representative organization. They were
given the most innocuous responsibilities, such as sports,
hiking, and rest camps. The real positions of power
always remained in Communist hands.

During 1948 the FDJ in the Soviet zone embarked on
a policy of full-scale support for the policies of the SED.
In the Western zones its groups continued their independent pose, and in Berlin the FDJ gave up its monopolistic
claims in return for a democratic cover when it agreed
to join with the three largest youth organizations in the
Western sectors—*Demokratische Jugendverband*—DJV
(Democratic Youth Organization), *Bund Deutscher Jugend*
(Federation of German Youth), and the Social Democratic
group, the *Falken*—in an all-Berlin body. This *rapproche-
ment* did not last beyond the middle of the year, how-

ever, because the FDJ closely followed the WFDY campaign against the West and the Marshall Plan.

With the hardening of the Soviet-Western split and the emergence of an East and West Germany, and an East and West Berlin, the FDJ gave up its attempts to establish a monopoly over German youth affairs. By infiltrating small meetings, and using the front technique of "preparatory committees," it did continue, however, to attempt to create a basis for united action with non-Communists. In April 1949 an "Action Committee" was formed at an inter-zonal meeting of youth representatives of all political parties, even though non-Communist youth organizations repudiated those who spoke for them. The "Action Committee" did not have a Communist majority, but was composed primarily of those who, for one reason or another, sought to cooperate with the Communists in hopes of achieving German unity. Given this situation, the committee was utilized by the Communists in classic fashion to create a "united front" in support of Communist policies.

This new policy also resulted in a more tolerant attitude on the part of the FDJ toward CDU youth who remained in the Soviet zone. If the FDJ was to have cooperation from non-Communists in the Western sectors of Germany, it had to at least create a façade of "above party" cooperation in its own sector. A formal statement of this new "national front" policy emerged at the third *Parlament* of the FDJ in June 1949, which, with its marches and pageantry, was described by one commentator as "a small edition of an imitation Nuremberg Party rally."[34] The FDJ was to build a "front of millions of youth."[35] The obviously partisan motivation behind these moves, and the realization by most young Germans that unification was an issue beyond their control, were causes for the failure of this drive. The non-Communists in the Western sectors simply refused to become the tools of a Soviet attempt to capture all Germany. The pretense of political neutrality and non-partisanship was finally abandoned in April 1957 when the FDJ became a recognized Communist organization, but the steady assertion of Communist control over the FDJ could be seen much earlier. The constitution approved at the first *Parlament* in June 1946 stipulated the formation of "voluntary" groups of young people in factories, schools, and according to place of residence. These were to be integrated by a hierarchical structure of local, county, district, and provincial committees. The guiding principle was to be voluntary participation, and delegates' meetings at each level were to be the highest governing bodies at these levels. Hidden behind these democratic aspects of the organization, however, were the realities of authoritarian control.

According to the constitution, the leadership at the various levels was to be elected by representative meetings. However, as these leaderships were to meet only periodically, they in turn elected a Secretariat to carry on day-to-day operations. A system of screening delegates to the various meetings, discussions with the SED, and the presentation of only one list of candidates made possible the careful pre-selection of both the leaderships and the Secretariats.

The constitution also provided that each youth body would direct the work of that immediately subordinate to it, and as the Communists made sure that they controlled the central executive of the FDJ, they established firm control over the entire organizational apparatus. A further constitutional provision required that only such persons be elected to leadership as supported the aims of the FDJ and had "appropriate character," and the Communists determined just what satisfied these requirements, and who fulfilled them.

The third congress (*Parlament*) of the FDJ in June 1949 approved a new constitution that further strengthened the control of the Communist leadership by abolishing secret elections and introducing a provision for the expulsion of members. Every member and all units were henceforth obliged to carry out the decisions of the governing bodies rapidly and conscientiously. The governing bodies were to submit all their decisions for approval by the next higher body, and their decisions could never contradict those of the central executive.

Interesting comparisons can be made between the FDJ and the *Hitler Jugend* (HJ). The latter, formed in 1926 as an arm of the Nazi Party before the assumption of power, acquired a monopoly position over youth affairs in Germany after 1933.[36] The familiar totalitarian process occurred, whereby sympathetic youth organizations were incorporated into the HJ and irreconcilable groups (especially church groups) were dissolved. This process of forming a single united National Socialist youth organization took until 1938, when the HJ was officially designated as the state youth organization.[37] The state delegated to the HJ certain functions ordinarily performed by government departments. In East Germany today, the FDJ is also occupied with many tasks of a governmental nature delegated to it by the Party.

Where, however, the FDJ is utilized to mobilize the youth for Party tasks, the HJ was far less concerned with this kind of thing. The primary emphasis in the HJ was leadership training, for it was primarily a school for Party cadres. Also, the activities of the HJ were primarily of a physical nature, and little time was "wasted" on intellectual debates and literary circles. But, very much like the FDJ, albeit with more success, Hitler's mobilization of youth was aimed at instilling everlasting obedience to the Party by molding character so as to make loyalty inherent. Alike in their totalitarian nature, the Nazi and East German Communist regimes differed (and differ) from democratic societies in their rejection of the concept of "ideological neutrality."

Unlike the HJ, however, the FDJ has been notoriously unable to attract the young people. Both before and after the erection of the Berlin Wall, about half of all those who fled to West Germany were under twenty-five. Not only has the East German regime failed to provide sufficient and varied opportunities for youth with adequate material rewards, and exercised a forbidding measure of control over youth activities, but it has also failed in the most basic area—ideological appeal. Any group of people, and youth in particular, can be persuaded to forego current rewards in the name of an ideal and the expectation of a better tomorrow. But the Communist regimes, East German and otherwise, have failed to convince youth that the ideal itself is worthwhile.

A RECORD OF FAILURE

By the early 1950s the Communist youth organizations of Eastern Europe had about 6 million young people in their ranks. Modeled on the Soviet Komsomol, and existing for the purpose of mobilizing youth behind the Communist regimes, the youth organizations concentrated on political indoctrination and assistance of the economic plans of the state. The summer work programs became an important element in the fulfillment of state plans.

Despite all efforts by the regimes, the continued inability of the youth organizations to interest the youth, or to meet their needs, has led to increasing dissatisfaction and disillusionment. Students were in the forefront of the 1956 upheavals in Eastern Europe. In Poland, and especially in Hungary, young people were leaders in the revolutionary activities of that year.[38] Although the Czechoslovak regime narrowly succeeded in avoiding a violent upheaval, the student demonstrations and meetings in the spring of 1956 caused considerable concern to the government and reflected deep unrest and discontent. And since 1960 Czechoslovak youth has again been particularly restive. Each May Day since 1962 there have been demonstrations, at times violent, in opposition to the state of affairs in Czechoslovakia.

The revolutionary events in Hungary and Poland forced the Communist regimes in those countries to completely reorganize their youth movements. In Hungary the students had taken the initiative in 1956 and formed their own independent organization, the United Association of

Hungarian University and College Students (MEFESZ),
an action that gave strong impetus to the revolutionary
upheaval in October-November, when the regime-spon-
sored youth organization, DISZ, fell apart from complete
lack of support. After the revolution had been suppressed,
the Kadar regime attempted unsuccessfully to infiltrate
and also set up its own youth groups, but these did not
take hold. In early 1957, therefore, the regime purged the
MEFESZ leadership, and the organization slowly withered
away. In March 1958 the government created two new
youth organizations—the *Kommunista Ifjusag Szövetsége*
—KISZ (Communist Youth League) for young workers,
and the EPOSZ for young peasants. The latter, however,
was apparently unsuccessful and appears to have been
abolished. Nor was much headway made in the universities, a stronghold of opposition to the regime.

In May 1958 the regime tightened its organizational
control over the youth and student movement by creating
a central organization similar to the Soviet KMOSSSR.
The National Council of Hungarian Youth was set up by
the Central Committee of KISZ to include all youth and
student organizations, and was placed under KISZ control
by installing a KISZ Central Committee member as Secretary-General.[39]

Nevertheless the apany of Hungarian youth persists.
Many students are overtly apolitical and stay outside
KISZ until it is time to leave high school. Then, in order
to gain admittance to the university, they join KISZ and
go through the motions of following the political line.
The regime has had to recognize this situation by relaxing
many of the restrictions on social, recreational, and
cultural life that existed in the Stalinist period.

In 1956, well before the critical events of the fall,
the youth of Poland was also becoming increasingly vocal
in its criticism of the state youth organization, the ZMP.[40]
The Gomulka regime later recognized the weakness of the
ZMP and took steps to dissolve it. In January 1957 it
acted to merge the youth groups that had sprung up
spontaneously in 1956 into the *Zwiazek Mlodziezy*

Socjalistycznej—ZMS (Union of Socialist Youth) as an affiliate of the Communist Party. But it' also allowed another spontaneously formed organization for work among rural youth, the *Zwiazek Mlodziezy Wiejskiej*—ZMW (Union of Peasant Youth) to continue to exist.

Poland is also the only Communist country where the Boy Scouts have been permitted to exist as an organization, although their name has been changed and their objectives are set by the Party. The Scouts were quickly infiltrated by the Communists after their resurrection as the *Zwiazek Harcerstwa Polskiege*—ZHP (Union of Polish Pioneers) after the liberation, and by 1948 had come under Communist domination. During the "thaw" of 1954 and 1955 the old Communist leaders were removed and there was a return to some of the pre-war apolitical activity. Under these conditions the ZHP had considerable appeal for those of Scouting age, and by 1956 the membership had risen to 1,500,000.[41] For a short period after 1956 the ZHP was not under Communist political control at all, but during 1957 a controversy took place within the leadership between those who wanted the Scouts to remain a non-political organization and those who wanted it to return to the status of a Party organization. As was to be expected, the latter group won, and by the summer of 1957 the Party had reasserted firm control. The result was a drastic drop in membership to less than 500,000.

All told, there are now five youth and student organizations in Poland:[42]

	Membership (February 1962)
Braves (7—11)	—
Union of Polish Pioneers—ZHP (11-18)	900,000
Union of Rural Youth—ZMW (16-21)	600,000
Union of Socialist Youth — ZMS (15-28)	600,000
Polish Students' Union—ZSP	100,000

The Union of Socialist Youth represents Poland in the World Federation of Democratic Youth, as does the

Polish Students' Union in the International Union of Students. The publications of the Polish youth movement are *Sztandar Mlodych* (daily), *Walka Mlodych* (monthly theoretical organ), *Dookota Swiata*, and *Nowa Wies* (the last two weeklies).

The firm measures taken by the authorities after 1956, including campaigns against "hooliganism," the increased use of university admittance as a lever of control, and the monopoly over recreational facilities, have again served to raise the membership in East European Communist youth organizations from the low point of 1956-1957. The increase in membership, however, does not reflect a sudden increase in enthusiasm on the part of youth, or a drastic change in the character of the youth organizations. Instead it signifies apathy, and a cynical acceptance of the realities of the present situation.

7/Chapter
Today and Tomorrow

The Communists have always paid keen attention to youth affairs, and have continually appealed to youth for support. Paradoxically, however, their success has been greater in those areas *not* under Communist control than in those that are.

Despite the fact that the Communist movement justifies itself as an all-embracing and logically coherent philosophical system, in practice Communist policies are subject to many erratic and irrational pressures. It is one thing for Communist leaders in the Soviet Union and elsewhere to develop a system by which the population is controlled and mobilized for Party-directed goals; it is quite another to implement this system smoothly and effectively. Contrary to the views of the "social engineers" of the far left, human nature, especially that of the younger generation, does not fit pliably into preconceived molds and patterns. The efforts of Communist parties to monopolize and control the activities of youth, to decide where, when, and how youth will be permitted outlets and to determine what are and are not legitimate goals for youth, have therefore tended to alienate youth.

It has been evident for some time that youth in the Communist countries is dissatisfied and growing more so. The Komsomol has not been able to win *active* support from the large mass of Soviet youth. Soviet young people exhibit intense patriotism, nationalism, and a general acceptance of the economic and social benefits of the Soviet system, but they are not devoted followers of the Soviet regime. While admiring Soviet material progress, they appear tired of the continual sacrifices demanded of them and are increasingly interested in enjoying the fruits of approaching affluence. Subordination of the individual to the state, the stifling of initiative, and repetitious political indoctrination have generated frustration, boredom, dissatisfaction, and apathy. All this has been reflected in growing juvenile delinquency, "hooliganism," and the spread among youth of "bourgeois ideology"—an interest in, even a worship of, things Western.

The desire of youth to partake of the "good life" is probably the basic reason why Communist regimes find it so difficult to persuade or coerce college graduates into taking jobs in the provinces, where they are most needed. Young people everywhere—especially the more educated ones—tend to gravitate toward cities, but in the Communist countries *all* the "good life" that exists is found only in the cities.

A craving for contact with the outside world is characteristic of current attitudes of youth under Communism. In the Soviet Union the most extreme manifestation of this search for things Western is the *stilyagi*—those young, and not so young, people who are dedicated to the quest for pleasure. Imitation of Western dress, speech, manners, and fads makes this small minority almost expatriates within their own society.

Most young people in the Soviet Union and the other Communist countries do, of course, substantially conform to the system. A small proportion probably believes wholeheartedly in the ideological dogmas of the Party. Some pay lip service to the system and to the organized youth movement in an effort to take advantage of the educational, vocational, and travel opportunities that accrue from Komsomol membership. The large mass of youth, however, remains apathetic and participates only because there is no alternative.

Dissatisfaction with the system is highest among university students and young intellectuals. Discussion groups on certain prohibited class topics are known to have been organized. Circulation of hand-written publications, even though such action is illegal, does take place. Official meetings have turned into forums of protest, and at times there have been public demonstrations and even riots.

Chairman Khrushchev's Twentieth Party Congress secret speech in February 1956 produced a deep impact on young people. A wave of protest against Party tutelage spread rapidly among youth. In Komsomol meetings, classrooms, and other gatherings open hostility toward the Party soon began to be felt, and was reflected in the concern shown by *Komsomolskaya Pravda* and *Molodoi Kommunist*. The situation deteriorated to the point where a special meeting of the Komsomol Central Committee was called in early 1957 to discuss means for improving Komsomol ideological work among youth.[1] During the latter part of that year and in early 1958 a number of young people were arrested and imprisoned on charges of spreading anti-Soviet propaganda. Yet while the Party has in the meantime succeeded in curbing the extremes of open criticism, the Pandora's box opened in 1956 can probably never again be closed.

Young professional people, with the writers in the vanguard, have been increasingly critical of restrictions imposed by the system on free expression and the free exchange of ideas. Young writers have been the leaders of the protests against the dogmatic approach to life that is so characteristic of Communist ideology. They are demanding new themes for literature, an abolition in fiction of propaganda themes, and an end to the rigidity of "socialist realism." The desire for more individual freedom—intellectual and physical—for an end to censorship, and for more travel abroad are the most frequently observed demands of young students and intellectuals.

On a broader scale, the large mass of young people, who are neither products of the higher educational system nor young intellectuals, are equally disillusioned. Although their horizons are not so high as to push them into protests and demands for more self-expression, they do have their own means of expressing discontent. The attitude that one does only enough to get by, that one does not "commit" himself, that one lets the "others" worry about plan fulfillment, is a result of the failure of the system to win the active allegiance of the young people. If they have no voice in either affairs of state or those of the Komsomol, there is obviously no incentive to become interested in these activities. Thus the continuing problem of the Soviet system is how to reconcile Party control over youth affairs with the need for *active* support and commitment from the mass of young people.

The reaction among young Communists to the removal of Nikita Khrushchev from power reflects another dilemma created by the liberalization since 1953. Terror, the arbitrary liquidation of competitors for state and Party power, and arbitrary leadership actions are no longer accepted, as they once were, as means for settling personal and political differences in the Communist world. An expectation of more democratic rule within and by the Communist parties, both those in power and those seeking power, has gradually developed, especially among the younger generation of Communists. Those young people in the Communist countries who today are in their mid-twenties or younger have spent their formative years completely in the era of liberalization. They know of Stalin and the "old methods" almost wholly from hearsay. The Stalinist days are not part of their own experience. They have been led to expect an evolution of Communist rule into something broader than existed under Stalin. The arbitrary manner in which Khrushchev was removed from power and the secretiveness surrounding the reasons for his dismissal, the immediate call for an explanation by many of the Communist parties, and the defensive reaction on the part of the new Soviet leaders are evidence of these changing expectations.

Among the more important expressions of displeasure with the manner of Khrushchev's dismissal was that by the French Communist student organization *Union Etudiante des Communistes* (UEC). On October 26, 1964, less than two weeks after Khrushchev's ouster, the National Committee of the UEC approved by more than a two-thirds majority a statement calling for a detailed explanation of the charges, to include the arguments used by Khrushchev in his defense. The French Communist student organization expressed particular concern about the effect Khrushchev's dismissal would have on the "image" of the Communist movement among students, and the future development of the decision-making process within the Communist movement. Communist student groups have, in fact, made some significant gains among students in the post-1956 period. A new image of Communism as a political movement emerged with the process of de-Stalinization. This has been fostered by Communist youth and student organizations whose policies have become more respectable in the eyes of the uncommitted, especially those in developing areas. The French student organization saw in the dismissal of Khrushchev an action that could well tarnish this new image and thus result in loss of support for Communist positions. Equally important, the dismissal of Khrushchev was seen by the French student organization as a step backward—away from the evolution of Communism as a system representing the will of all "peace-loving, working-class" elements, and towards a reintroduction of discredited and publicly condemned Stalinist methods.

The National Committee statement posed two extremely important questions: What part do members of the Communist Party of the Soviet Union, and the Soviet people in general, play in making decisions in the Soviet Union? How could such a step take place, eight years after the changes in outlook that had resulted from the process of de-Stalinization? The fact that these questions are even asked, and demands made for satisfactory answers, clearly reflects these changed expectations on the part of young Communists. No longer do they accept the Stalinist assumption that one man can or should rule the party. The question of what share they, as young Communists and potential future leaders, can have in determining the course of developments within the Communist movement has become more and more important to them.

This problem of expectations exists within Communist youth and student ranks both inside and outside the Communist orbit. The Communist parties in power must evoke a sense of commitment from youth, and the problem of young Communist functionaries is how to keep that commitment alive. Inside the bloc, the career expectations of young Communists—in terms of personal security, possibilities for advancement, opportunity to express varying views, and participation in the decision-making process within the party—have been rising for more than a decade. In the Communist movements that are not in power, the degree of commitment from the young Communists is directly related to their expectations of exercising influence over the nature of the "new society" formed after the Communists take power. Surely the younger generation of Communists, having been led to expect some basic changes in the operational code of their own and other Communist parties, must have experienced a letdown and disappointment, if not actual disillusionment, as a result of the manner in which Khrushchev was removed. Some may have accepted the change cynically as just the "same old thing" and, as good "opportunists," not been too concerned. The reaction called forth, however, indicates that these were in a distinct minority.

The ouster of Khrushchev, and the reaction to it, provides a further example of the basic problem of Communist policy towards the younger generation: how to reconcile the desire and need of the party leaders for an active commitment from youth with the demand of the system for a monopoly of political power by the party. The more the party changes so as to increase the expectations of the young people, the more will it win their support. At the same time, however, the party will be eroding its own monopoly of power. Expectations have been that the exercise of power in the Soviet Union would be broadened from that of one man to the party as a whole. Although this may not have occurred in the Soviet Union, certainly the arena for decision-making seems to have been broadened to include the Central Committee. Once, however, the arena for decision-making is broadened, it is difficult to see how the process can be halted without recourse to some of the methods previously used to guarantee one-man rule.

Juvenile delinquency has been increasing since World War II in both Communist and non-Communist countries, and for much the same reasons. Modern industrial life, and congested living and working quarters, have broken down many traditional standards of conduct, and have provided a mobility—from farm to city, and from city to city—that has not heretofore existed. Add to this frequent breakdowns of family life, recurring difficulties of college graduates in finding jobs at their proper level, and the general deterioration of social values, and it is little wonder that more and more youths have turned to various forms of anti-social behavior. In the Communist countries the lack of identification with the regime, and the refusal of the Party to consider the goals and decisions of youth apart from Party goals, have been important factors in the rise of juvenile delinquency.

Communist theory has it that such delinquency is the result of the social injustice inherent in capitalist society. Thus juvenile delinquency in Communist countries is explained as resulting from Western influences such as crime magazines and novels and radio broadcasts. The Communists, therefore, say that when their educational system has succeeded in producing the "new socialist man" this anti-social behavior will cease. Yet the creation of this ideal "new socialist man" still seems as far away as ever.

An obvious paradox emerges when one examines the approach of the Communist regimes to the problem of controlling delinquency. A central role in attempting to overcome anti-social behavior is assigned to the Communist youth organizations. But these youth organizations are probably the least influential of all the forces in a Communist society. "Criticized, boycotted, and, at the crucial moment, scuttled by their own members (in Poland and Hungary in 1956), there is little to suggest that they have succeeded in gaining a real hold in recent years."[2]

A related concern of the Soviet and other Communist regimes has been to prevent the spread of "bourgeois ideology" among young people. From the early thirties until the mid-fifties the Soviet population was effectively isolated from outside influences. However, with the opening of the Soviet Union to foreign visitors in the mid-fifties, and the limited relaxation of controls on foreign travel by Soviet citizens, the exposure of Soviet youth to Western ideas and influences increased rapidly. The World Youth Festival in Moscow in 1957, the U. S. National Exhibition in 1959, and activities under the cultural exchange agreements signed between the United States and the Soviet Union since 1958 have all increased contacts between Soviet youth and the outside world.[3] Tours of athletes, orchestras, individual artists, exhibits, and the presence of Western students at Soviet universities have all contributed to the rise in "bourgeois" influences on the young people of the Soviet Union.

In Eastern Europe the problems of the influence of "bourgeois ideology" are both of more and less concern. On the one hand, most of the regimes have found it necessary as a result of "de-stalinization" to allow far wider latitude for cultural contacts with the West than has been the case in the U.S.S.R. This pressure has been complemented by the traditional ties of many East European nations with the West. One finds Western-style coffee houses, modern jazz, the "twist," many modern Western films, and the growing influence of Western architecture and interior decor. At the same time, however, the decisions to allow more freedom in these areas have provided a "safety valve" through which discontent is allowed to escape into politically less damaging channels.

Within the Soviet Union the emphasis of the Party on using the youth, rather than on serving them, has made the Komsomol an unappealing and uninspiring institution. In the nineteen twenties the Komsomol was concerned primarily with consolidating its monopoly position over youth activities, the problem of Party control over the Komsomol, and then with the intra-Party struggle. After the assertion of firm control over Party and State by Stalin in the late twenties, the Komsomol was turned primarily to economic tasks. During World War II military needs predominated. More recently, at its April 1962 Congress it was called upon to mobilize the energies of young people for the creation of the material and technical base of Communism; to intensify its ideological work in the effort to rear the "new socialist man"; to work more actively to strengthen the ties between school and life;[4] to strengthen friendship and cooperation with world youth; and to do "everything possible to reinforce and protect the unity and solidarity of the mighty socialist camp . . . ."[5]

The liberalization of the Soviet system since the death of Stalin has both eased and increased the pressure for change generated by youth. By providing more outlets for youthful interests the government has provided an outlet for youthful discontent. On the other hand, the more room youth finds for self-expression and the more it expects from the regime, the more difficult it will be for the Party to channel the interests of youth into those directions most desired by the Party leadership. And if this is a serious problem in the Soviet Union, it is considerably more so in the East European countries, where the Communist regimes have been least successful in appealing to youth, and are most troubled by the consequences of the growing alienation of youth from the system.

Out of power, the Communists enjoy the advantage of not bearing responsibility for their actions and policies—they are thus free to criticize and attack, offer and promise. Whereas in the Communist countries it is the Communist regime that must take the responsibility for any inability of the system to satisfy the demands of the people, in those areas where the Communists are not in power they can, and do, feel free to adopt as critical and irresponsible an attitude as they wish. Their objective is power, and any action that furthers this objective is, from their point of view, a desirable one. Lack of responsibility is thus an open door to license.

The radical slogans and programs of the Communists out of power, whose main interest is in destroying the *status quo*, and who have never had to be judged on the basis of their performance, have often found considerable support among youth, as indeed they did in many of the Communist countries in the period before the Communist assumption of power.

Prior to 1945 the Soviet Union was the only Communist state. The active Communist youth movements outside the Soviet Union were confined primarily to Western Europe, and were subordinated to the interests of Soviet foreign policy. Although the Communist Youth International claimed membership from a large number of countries, most affiliated organizations in Eastern Europe and in the non-European areas were either illegal or very small. With the creation of new Communist states in Eastern Europe and the Far East after World War II, the new national Communist youth organizations were formed on the Komsomol model. A new international youth organization was formed on a more sophisticated level to replace the CYI, and a separate international organization for students was created. The subordination of these Communist front organizations to Stalin's foreign policy led to their decline and isolation. New, more moderate lines of policy instituted by Khrushchev laid the basis for a recovery of prestige and influence. With the decline of

British, French, and other colonial powers and the creation of a large number of new states, the opportunities for expansion and growth of the Communist youth movement rose correspondingly. Similarly, worsening economic, political, and social conditions in Latin America in the late nineteen fifties, as well as the rise of Castro, have aided the Communists considerably. A negative development for Communist front activities has been the growth of the schism within the international Communist movement. If the current trend continues, the ability of the Communists to capitalize on the opportunities open to them in the non-Communist world will remain seriously limited.

Apart from the Sino-Soviet split, however, the future of the Communist youth movement will depend on two fundamental questions: will the Communist regimes take steps to modify their system so as to provide a degree of self-expression for youth adequate to win youth's allegiance and *active* support; and will the crises, tensions, and instabilities in the non-Communist world, especially in the developing countries of the "third area," be allowed by both the indigenous leaders and the leaders of the Western democracies to reach the point where the frustrations of the majority of the young people lead them to turn to more radical solutions? To the extent that the Communists in power continue to limit the self-expression of youth, their regimes will continue to forfeit youth's support. To the extent that democratic solutions, which include a rapid rate of economic progress, are found for the needs of the developing countries, the opportunities for the Communists will remain limited. The successes of the international Communist youth organizations in recent years reflect an awareness by the Communist leaders of the realities of the international scene and a willingness to maintain a certain flexibility in approach. This represents a significant change from the dogmatic attitude of the Communist Youth International during the nineteen twenties and thirties.

The Communists rightly believe that crisis, tension,

and instability create opportunities for radical (Communist) solutions, and they have continually sought to take advantage of, and intensify, those forces that tend to create such conditions. They find considerable hope in the anti-imperialism of the newly independent peoples of Asia and Africa. The Communists see a further source of exploitable tension in the impatience of many leaders in the developing nations for rapid economic development. The trend toward one-party states with a wide degree of state control over the economy may, they think, lead these countries to turn to the Soviet model.

While these sources of instability represent possible opportunities for Communist exploitation, the question arises as to who specifically will profit most from them. In view of the seemingly genuine change in Soviet methods of expansion, which now rely less on violence and more on peaceful pressures for change, the observation has been made that it may well be Communist China, with its insistence on revolutionary opposition to the *status quo*, that will make the greatest appeal to the youth in the "third area."

In many areas of the non-Communist world today the Communists are having considerable success in winning the allegiance of the youth, especially the students. In Latin America, for instance, where the democratic forces of reform and progress are growing, but are still relatively weak, the Communists assert themselves to be the only real force for change. Elsewhere, in countries that have only recently won their freedom from colonial rule, new and conservative native leaderships have often taken power and, in effect, merely substituted themselves for the former European rulers. The Communists have not been slow to play on the opposition of youth to this development.

Yet despite the growing success of the Communists the young people in most developing areas remain primarily nationalist, and support leaders and bodies such as Nasser, Sukarno, the Indian Congress Party, Bourguiba, Ben Bella, and the other nationalist leaders and bodies of independent Africa and Asia. The real danger, however, lies in the fact that, while the present strength of the Communists is not alarmingly great, the pressure is on the democratic elements rather than on the Communists. The democratic elements must solve, by democratic means and through democratic institutions, the tremendous social, economic, and political problems in the developing nations in the face of tremendous pressures for easy and rapid solutions. The Communists can sit back and wait for what they hope will be the failute of the democratic elements.

The recognition by the Communist youth and student front organizations that they had more to gain than to lose by presenting a less dogmatic and autocratic appearance has enabled them to overcome their organizational weaknesses. Following the immediate post-World War II years, when the WFDY and the IUS could legitimately claim to speak for a sizable portion of the world's young people, the Communist fronts under Stalin were reduced to distinct minority organizations that "represented" only the youth in the Communist bloc countries. The emphasis in WFDY and IUS activities on Asia, Africa, the Middle East, and Latin America from 1955 on, and the acceptance of non-Communist, neutralist youth and student organizations into the WFDY and the IUS, has enabled these organizations to grow into a world force that should not be underestimated. A further success for the Communists has resulted from their capture of, or exertion of decisive influence on, a number of representative student organizations that are members of the non-Communist International Student Conference. This has had the effect of introducing a disturbing influence into the deliberations of international democratic student organizations, as well as forcing the ISC further to the left.

There will always be young people; there will always be that stage of human development in which curiosity, questioning, hopes, yearnings, idealism, are uppermost. Concerned with finding and asserting themselves, young people are the least subject to control and the most resentful of authority. Self-expression and self-assertiveness require freedom and independence. So long as the Communists retain monopolistic control over all aspects of those societies under their control, so long will they fail in their efforts to win the allegiance and *active* support of, and commitment from, their young people.

Appendix 1

MEMBERSHIP OF THE IUS

Because of the unwillingness of the Communist front organizations to publish details concerning their membership, compilation of accurate membership lists is extremely difficult. The IUS is considerably more open in this regard than the WFDY, and a reasonably complete list is set forth below. It should be noted, however, that inaccuracies may unavoidably exist. In some cases the listed member organization is the representative student organization in the country; in other cases it is only one of the minority student groups in the country. Furthermore, in some cases, such as the Dominican Republic, the student organization listed is the representative organization, and formally a member of the IUS, but the IUS leadership accords only the minority faction within the national organization the right to representation in the IUS organs. In Colombia, the listed IUS member organization has been long defunct, there being no representative national student union in that country. Some organizations have joined the IUS only as associate members. Where such is known to be the case, an asterisk* has been placed before the listed organization.

A reasonably accurate membership list for the WFDY is almost impossible to compile, particularly since in many countries there are a large number of youth organizations of all sizes and nature recognized as WFDY members. At the end of 1963 the WFDY claimed 101 million individual members in more than 100 countries.

Africa (Portuguese)	Union Générale des Etudiants d'Afrique Noire Sous Domination Coloniale Portugaise (UGEAN)
Africa (West)	Union Générale des Etudiants d'Afrique Occidentale (UGEAO)—Dakar
	West African Students Union in the United Kingdom (WASU)
Africa (West and Central)	Fédération des Etudiants d'Afrique ˎNoire en France (FEANF)
Albania	Union de la Jeunesse du Travail d'Albanie, Section Etudiante
Algeria	Union Nationale des Etudiants d'Algérie (UNEA)
Argentina	Federacion Universitaria Argentina (FUA)
Belgium	*Vereniging der Vlaamse Studenten (VVS)
	*Mouvement des Etudiants Universitaires Belges d'Expression Française (MUBEF)
Bolivia	Confederacion Universitaria Boliviana
Brazil	Uniao Nacional dos Estudantes do Brasil (UNEB)
Bulgaria	Student Council of the Dimitrovski Kommunisticheski Mladezhki Suiuz
Burma	All-Burma Federation of Student Unions (name unknown)
Cambodia	Union des Etudiants Khmer (UEK)
Cameroons	Union Nationale des Etudiants du Kamerun (UNEK)
Ceylon	Ceylon National Union of Students
	*Ceylon University Students Federation
Chile	*Union de Federaciones Universitarias de Chile (UFUCh)
Chinese People's Republic	All-China Students Federation

Colombia	Consejo Estudiantil Colombiano Universitario (UNEC) (no longer in existence but still listed by the IUS as a member; the communist-controlled student organization is the Federación Universitaria Nacional-FUN)
Congo (Brazzaville)	*Union Générale des Etudiants de Congo (UGEC)
Cuba	Federacion Estudiantil Universitaria (FEU)
Cyprus	Union of Cypriot Students
Czechoslovakia	Student Council of the Ceskoslovensky Svaz Mladzhe
Dominican Republic	Federacion de Estudiantes Dominicanos
Ecuador	Federacion Estudiantil Universitaria de Ecuador (FEUE) (dissolved by the Ecuadorian government in March 1964)
El Salvador	*Associacion General de Estudiantes Universitarios Salvadorenos (AGEUS)
Ethiopia	National Union of Ethiopian Students
France	*Union Nationale des Etudiants de France (UNEF)
German Democratic Republic	Freie Deutsche Jugend (Student Section) (FDJ)
Ghana	National Union of Ghana Students (NUGS)
Guadeloupe	Association Générale des Etudiants Guadeloupéens (AGEG)
Guiana, French	Union des Etudiants Guyanais
Haiti	*Union Nationale des Etudiants Haitiens
Hungary	National Committee of Hungarian Student Organizations
India	All-India Student Federation
Indonesia	*Perserikatan Perhimpunan Mahasiswa Indonesia (PPMI)
Iran	Tehran University Students' Union
Iraq	General Union of Students in the Iraqi Republic (GUSIR) *Iraqi Students Society in the U.K.
Japan	All-Japan Federation of Student Autonomies (Zengakuren)

Jordan	(unknown)
Kenya	Student Union of Royal College
Korea, North	Korean Students Committee
Kurdistan	*Kurdish Students' Society in Europe
Lebanon	*Union Générale des Etudiants du Liban
Liberia	Liberian National Union of Students
Madagascar (Malagasy Republic)	Association des Etudiants d'Origine Malagache
	*Association Générale des Etudiants de Madagascar
Martinique	Association Générale des Etudiants de la Martinique
Mexico	Confederacion de Jovenes Mexicanos (CJM)
Mongolia	Union of Mongolian Students
Morocco	*Union Nationale des Etudiants de Maroc (UNEM)
Nicaragua	*Centro Universitario de la Universidad Nacional
Nigeria	National Union of Nigerian Students (NUNS)
Palestine (Arab refugees)	General Union of Palestine Students (GUPS)
Panama	Union de Estudiantes Universitarios (UEU)
Peru	*Federacion de Estudiantes del Peru (FEP)
Poland	Zrzeszenie Studentów Polskich (ZSP)
Puerto Rico	Federacion de Universitarios Pro Independencia (FUPI)
Réunion	Students' Union of Réunion
Romania	Uniunea Asociatiilor Studentilor din Republica Populara Romina
Sierra Leone	Students Representative Council of Fourrah Bay College
South Vietnam (Viet Cong)	Union des Etudiants pour la Libération du Vietnam du Sud
Sudan	Khartoum University Students' Union (KUSU)
Tanzania	Tanganyika: University Students' Union
	Zanzibar: All-Zanzibar Student Union
Tunisia	Union Générale des Etudiants de Tunisie

Uganda	Makerere College Guild
U.S.S.R.	Studenchiskii Soviet SSSR (Student Council of the U.S.S.R.)
Venezuela	Federacion de Centros Universitarios
Vietnam, North	Union Nationale des Etudiants de Vietnam

Appendix 2

FESTIVAL ATTENDANCE

(excluding host country participants)

Year	Location	Persons	Countries
1947	Prague, Czechoslovakia	12,000	71
1949	Budapest, Hungary	10,000	82
1951	East Berlin, Germany	23,000	104
1953	Bucharest, Romania	27,000	110
1955	Warsaw, Poland	28,000	114
1957	Moscow, U.S.S.R.	30,000	131
1959	Vienna, Austria	14,000	108
1962	Helsinki, Finland	12,000	135

Source: *Youth and Freedom*, Volume V, No. 4, p. 11.

Notes

INTRODUCTION

1. Leo Gruliow and Charlotte Saikowski, *Current Soviet Policies: IV* (New York and London: Columbia University Press, 1962), p. 25.
2. *Ibid.*
3. A. Afonin, *A Short History of the Young Communist League of the Soviet Union* (Moscow-Leningrad: Cooperative Publishing Society of Foreign Workers in the U.S.S.R., 1934), pp. 11-12.
4. V. I. Lenin, *The Young Generation* (New York: International Publishers, 1940), pp. 12-13.
5. *Sbornik Sotsial-Demokrat*, No. 2 (December 1916), pp. 76-77.
6. O. Ryvkin, *Ocherki po istorii VLKSM* (Sketches from the History of the All-Union Leninist Communist Union of Youth) (3d ed.; Moscow: Ogiz, Molodaia Gvardiia, 1933), pp. 59-61.
7. Afonin, p. 23.
8. Lenin, pp. 26-48.

The Birth of the Communist Youth Movement (1915 - 1925)

1. See Willi Münzenberg, *Die sozialistischen Jugendorganisa-*

tionen während des Krieges (Berlin: Verlag Junge Garde, 1919) for a summary history of the Socialist youth movement up to 1919. Tendentious but useful.

2. The discussion in this chapter of the Socialist youth movement during World War I, and the subsequent development of the Communist Youth International up to 1924, is taken from the author's Ph.D. dissertation, "The Origins and Development of the Communist Youth International: 1914-1924," now in preparation for the Russian Institute, Columbia University.

3. There is no adequate biography of Münzenberg. His autobiographical work, *Die Dritte Front* (1930), discusses his participation in the Socialist and Communist youth movements up to 1921. Brief discussions of his career and character are in R. N. Carew-Hunt, "Willi Muenzenberg," *International Communism* (St. Antony's Papers, No. 9; Carbondale, Ill.: Southern Illinois University Press, 1960); Arthur Koestler, *The Invisible Writing* (New York: Macmillan, 1954), pp. 205-212; and Ruth Fischer, *Stalin and German Communism* (Cambridge, Mass.: Harvard University Press, 1948), pp. 610-614.

4. *Sie ist nicht tot! Bericht über die internationale Konferenz der sozialistischen Jugendorganisationen 1915 zu Bern* (Zurich, 1915).

5. *Unter dem roten Banner; Bericht über den ersten Kongress der Kommunistischen Jugend-Internationale* (Berlin, 1920).

6. See footnote 2 and *Zu neuer Arbeit; Bericht vom II Kongress der KJI abgehalten vom 14. bis 21. Juli 1921 in Moskau* (Berlin, 1921).

7. See *Decisions of the Third Congress of the Communist International* (London: Communist Party of Great Britain, 1921), pp. 119-122, for the congress decisions on the youth movement.

8. The only historical studies that have been made of the Communist youth movement in the Soviet Union are those by Soviet authors. From the early nineteen-thirties to the late fifties very little was published by the Soviets on the history of the youth movement in Russia. In recent years, however, a considerable number of memoirs, reminiscences,

histories of local and provincial youth organizations, and other works on the youth movement have appeared. The official Soviet view of the Komsomol is in the *Bolshaia Sovietskaia Entsyklopedia* (2d ed.), Vol. 9, pp. 330-347, and in a recently published history, *Leninskii Komsomol; ocherki po istorii VLKSM* (2d, rev. ed.; Molodaia Gvardiia, 1961). The major non-Communist works are Ralph Fisher, *Pattern for Soviet Youth* (New York: Columbia University Press, 1959), which is not a history, but rather a very useful analysis of the Congresses of the Komsomol in which the author has attempted to ascertain "the pattern of attitudes and behavior which the regime, in and through the Komsomol, sought to impose upon Soviet youth," and Merle Fainsod, "The Komsomol—Youth under Dictatorship," Chapter 9 of his *How Russia is Ruled* (rev. ed.; Cambridge, Mass.: Harvard University Press, 1963). In Fisher's notes (p. 296), he discusses a number of Communist accounts of Komsomol history. In this chapter I have relied on Ryvkin, *op. cit.*, for the formation of the Komsomol. Other useful sources are Afonin, *op. cit.*, and P. Kruzhin, "The Youth Movement in the Soviet Union," *Youth in the Soviet Union* (Munich: Institute for the Study of the USSR, 1959).

9. *KPSS o komsomole i molodezhi* (The CPSU on the Komsomol and the Youth) (Moscow: Molodaia Gvardiia, 1957), pp. 6-7.

10. From the resolution of the party congress, *ibid.*, pp. 33-34.

11. *Ibid.*, pp. 35-37.

12. Quoted in Fisher, pp. 16-17.

13. See Fisher, pp. 80-84.

14. *Ibid.*, pp. 53-56.

15. See Fisher, Appendix B.

The Stalinization of the Communist Youth Movement (1925-1941)

1. *International Press Correspondence*, Vol. 8, No. 60 (September 6, 1928), pp. 1054-1056.

2. The events within the Soviet Communist party are described in detail in Leonard Schapiro, *The Communist Party of the Soviet Union* (New York: Random House, 1960).

3. *IPC*, Vol. 6, No. 64 (September 30, 1926), p. 1098, and No. 65 (October 7, 1926), p. 1117.

4. *IPC*, Vol. 9, No. 5 (January 25, 1929), p. 86.

5. *IPC*, Vol. 9, No. 5 (January 25, 1929), p. 86.

6. *IPC*, Vol. 10, No. 52 (November 20, 1930), p. 1076.

7. See Fisher, *op. cit.*, pp. 113-127 and 143-157, for the Komsomol and the party controversies.

8. *Lenin i Stalin o molodezhi* (Moscow: Molodaia Gvardiia, 1938), pp. 270-273.

    Fisher, *op. cit.*, Appendix B and p. 129. All membership figures for the Komsomol in this study have been taken from Fisher.

10. *Ustav Vsesoiuznovo Leninskovo Kommunisticheskovo Soiuza Molodezhi* (Moscow: Izdatci'stvo TsK VLKSM "molodaia Gvardiia," 1940), p. 1.

11. From the Party regulations adopted at the 18th Party Congress (March 1939): *KPSS o komsomole i molodezhi, op. cit.*, p. 297.

12. *The Young Communist International between the Fourth and Fifth Congresses, 1924-28* (London: Communist Party of Great Britain, 1928), p 24.

13. *International of Youth* (London) No. 1, 1925, pp. 4-6.

14. *The Young Communist International . . . 1924-28, op. cit.*, p. 25.

15. *IPC*, Vol. 8, No. 60 (September 6, 1928), pp. 1054-1056.

16. For the activities of the Comintern in the twenties and thirties see the works of Borkenau, Nollau, and Seton-Watson cited in the bibliography.

17. *IPC*, Vol. 6, No. 39 (May 6, 1926), p. 608.

18. *IPC*, Vol. 6, No. 35 (April 29, 1926), p. 541.

19. *IPC*, Vol. 6, No. 28 (April 15, 1926), p. 429.

20. See Carew-Hunt, *op. cit.*, p. 76.

21. *The Young Communist International . . . 1924-28*, p. 13.

22. *IPC*, Vol. 9, No. 39 (August 16, 1929), pp. 834-835.

23. *IPC*, Vol. 8, No. 80 (November 16, 1928), p. 1508.

24. *IPC*, Vol. 13, No. 11 (March 9, 1933), p. 278.

25. *IPC*, Vol. 13, No. 32 (July 21, 1933), p. 708.

26. *Ibid.*

27. *IPC*, Vol. 13, No. 44 (October 6, 1933), pp. 973-974.

28. *IPC*, Vol. 15, No. 50 (October 5, 1935), p. 1271.
29. *Ibid.*
30. *The Day Is Ours! Report of M. Woolf to the 6th World Congress of the Young Communist International* (London: n.d.), p. 9.
31. *Ibid.*, p. 14.
32. *IPC*, Vol. 16, No. 6 (January 25, 1936), p. 171.
33. *Ibid.*, p. 173.
34. *IPC*, Vol. 16, No. 4 (March 28, 1936), p. 441.
35. *IPC*, Vol. 16, No. 19 (April 18, 1936), p. 514; for the joint statement on YSL-YCL unity in Spain see *Internatsional Molodezhi*, No. 4 (April 1936), pp. 19-20.
36. *Clarity* (theoretical organ of the Young Communist League, U. S. A.), Vol. 1, No. 3 (Fall Issue, 1940).
37. *Ibid.*, Vol. 2, No. 1 (Spring Issue, 1941), pp. 5-6.
38. *IPC*, Vol. 15, No. 5 (February 2, 1935), p. 145.
39. *IPC*, Vol. 16, No. 36 (August 8, 1936), p. 979.
40. *Youth Plans a New World; Being the Official Record of the First World Youth Congress (Geneva, 31 August-6 September 1936)*, p. 11.
41. *Ibid.*, p. 148.
42. *World News and Views,* Vol. 18, No. 39 (August 13, 1938), p. 921.
43. George Philip Rawick, "The New Deal and Youth: The Civilian Conservation Corps, the National Youth Administration, and the American Youth Congress" (Unpublished Ph.D. dissertation, University of Wisconsin, 1957), p. 284. The following discussion of the American Youth Congress relies heavily on this source.
44. *Ibid.*, p. 288.
45. *Ibid.*, p. 290.
46. *Ibid.*, pp. 294-295.
47. *Ibid.*, p. 295.
48. *Ibid.*, p. 296.
49. *Ibid.*, p. 336.
50. *Ibid.*, pp. 308, 331.
51. *Ibid.*, p. 311.
52. *Ibid.*, p. 332.
53. *Ibid.*, p. 341.

54. *Ibid.*
55. *New York Times*, August 24, 1938, p. 38.
56. *IPC*, Vol. 18, No. 42 (September 3, 1938), pp. 981-982. The text of the "Peace Pact" is also in the *New York Times*, August 24, 1938, p. 23.
57. *New York Times*, August 23, 1938, p. 19.
58. Rawick, *op. cit.*, p. 347.
59. *Clarity*, Vol. 2, No. 2 (Summer Issue, 1941).
60. *Ibid.*, Vol. 3, No. 3 (Summer Issue, 1942), p. 3.
61. *Ibid.*
62. *Ibid.*, Vol. 4, No. 1 (Spring Issue, 1943), p. 8.
63. Martin Ebon, *World Communism Today* (New York: Whittlesey House, 1948), pp. 457-458.
64. *Daily Worker* (New York), April 3, 1943.

The International Communist Youth and Student Movements in the Post-War Period (1945-1953)

1. Werner Lamberz and Klaus Jeutner, *Vereint mit 87 Millionen* (East Berlin: Verlag Neues Leben, 1960), pp. 31-38, and *Report of the World Youth Conference*, October 31-November 9, 1945, by the United States Delegation (New York: n.d.).
2. *Report of the World Youth Conference . . .*, Appendix 4.
3. *Ibid.*
4. *Ibid.*, p. 2. In 1945 two representatives from the World Youth Council were accredited to the international conference in San Francisco at which the United Nations was founded.
5. *Ibid.*, Appendix 2, resolution (d).
6. *Ibid.*, Appendix 6.
7. For the development of the IUS see Peter T. Jones, *The History of U. S. National Student Association Relations with the International Union of Students, 1945-1956* (Philadelphia: Foreign Policy Research Institute, University of Pennsylvania, 1956; 135 pp.); Ralph Blumenau, *Communists and Students.* (London: Batchworth Press, 1954; 40 pp.); and Nils M. Apeland, *World Youth and the Communists* (London: Phoenix House, 1958), pp. 22-27.
8. Jones, p. 7.
9. *Ibid.*, pp. 16-18.

10. Apeland, p. 31.
11. See Chapter 6 for a discussion of the World Youth Festivals.
12. See J. M. Mackintosh, *Strategy and Tactics of Soviet Foreign Policy* (New York and London: Oxford University Press, 1963; 353 pp.) for a discussion of Soviet foreign policy at this time.
13. See Gerd Friedrich, *Die Freie Deutsche Jugend* (Cologne: Rote Weissbücher, 1950), pp. 30-31, for a discussion of the Second WFDY Council session.
14. Apeland, p. 26.
15. Jones, pp. 36-37.
16. For the British position see Blumenau, p. 11.
17. See Jones.
18. Ellis's letter of resignation to the IUS is quoted in full in Jones, pp. 52-56.
19. Jones, p. 59.
20. Blumenau, p. 14.
21. After the Austrian State Treaty in 1955, the Communist front organizations were asked to leave the country as the Austrian government sought to practice a strict neutrality. The WFDY moved to Budapest.
22. *Vsemirnyi Festival Molodezhi v Prage* (World Youth Festival in Prague) (Prague: Orbis, 1948), p. 5.
23. See Ruth T. McVey, *The Calcutta Conference and the South East Asian Uprisings* (Ithaca, N.Y.: Department of Far Eastern Studies, Cornell University, 1958).
24. Jones, p. 36; Mackintosh, pp. 54-55.
25. Jones, p. 69.
26. Blumenau, p. 15.
27. *Ibid.* Italics added.
28. *Ibid.*, pp. 19-20. Italics added.
29. *Ibid.*
30. See Blumenau, p. 20; Apeland, p. 35.
31. Blumenau, pp. 23-27.
32. *Ibid.*, p. 24.
33. Blumenau, pp. 28-37; Jones, pp. 75-76.
34. See *Youth and Freedom*, Vol. 5, No. 3, pp. 1-4; Jones, pp. 80-81; Apeland, pp. 40-41.
35. Apeland, p. 39.

The Youth and Student Fronts Under Khrushchev
(1953-1964).

1. See Mackintosh, pp. 72-87.

2. Blumenau, p. 39.

3. *International Union of Students, IX Annual Council Meeting, Moscow, 20-27 August, 1954.* (International Union of Students, 1954), pp. 14-16.

4. *What's New in the Student Movement? How Can Unity Be Achieved?* (Prague: International Union of Students, 1956).

5. *World Student News*, No. 1, 1957.

6. *International Union of Students, . . . Council . . . . 1954*, p. 8.

7. UGEAO (West Africa), FEANF (French Africa), UGEMA (Algeria), CUB (Bolivia), ABFSU (Burma), CUSF (Ceylon), UFUCh (Chile), FEU (Cuba), FEUE (Ecuador), GUSIR (Iraq), *Zengakuren* (Japan), LNUS (Liberia), UNEM (Morocco), CUUN (Nicaragua), GUPS (Palestine), SRC (Sierra Leone), KUSU (Sudan), UGET (Tunisia), FCU (Venezuela), UGEAN (Portuguese Africa), FUA (Argentina), UNEB (Brazil), PPMI (Indonesia), NUNS (Nigeria), ECEC (Congo, Leopoldville).

8. Jones, p. 97.

9. *International Union of Students, . . . Council . . . 1954*, pp. 19-21.

10. *Ibid.*

11. *Ibid.*, p. 20.

12. In order to facilitate cooperation with the non-Communists, the IUS created an allegedly autonomous body, the University Sports Council, to coordinate its international sports activities.

13. *International Union of Students, . . . Council . . . 1954*, p. 13.

14. *X Annual Council Meeting of International Union of Students, Sofia, 26-31 August 1955* (Prague: International Union of Students, 1955), p. 16.

15. See *World Student News*, No. 3-4 (March-April), 1955.

16. Jones, p. 101.

17. From the preface to the IUS-UNEF proposal as quoted in Jones, p. 108.

18. *World Youth*, No. 1, 1958, p. 3.
19. The UGET (Tunisia) was founded in 1953, and while allied with Bourguiba and the Neo-Destour Party, exercises considerable independence. The UNEA (Algeria) was founded in 1955 as the UGEMA, and is associated with the FLN in the same manner as the Tunisian student organization is with the Neo-Destour. The divisions in the FLN have been reflected in the student movement, with the formation of an anti-Ben Bella organization, General Union of Democratic Algerian Students (UBEDA).
20. *Radio Moscow*, March 24, 1960.
21. See *Youth and Freedom*, Vol. 4, No. 3-4, pp. 1-9.
22. *Ibid.*, p. 6.
23. *News Features*, Vol. V, No. 4 (April 20, 1964), p. 4.
24. Category A includes those organizations that have a basic interest in most of the activities of the ECOSOC, and are closely linked with the economic or social life of the areas they represent; Category B includes those organizations that have a special sphere but are more specifically concerned with only a few of the fields of activity covered by ECOSOC.
25. United Nations, Economic and Social Council, *Official Records*, Eleventh Session, 395th Meeting.
26. United Nations Educational, Scientific, and Cultural Organization, Records of the General Conference, Seventh Session, Paris 1952, *Resolutions*, p. 22.
27. *East African Standard*, February 8, 1964.
28. See *Youth and Communism*, Vol. 2, No. 1 (March 1959).
29. *Moscow Radio*, December 19, 1958.
30. *World Student News*, No. 8, 1960.
31. *Youth and Freedom*, Vol. V, No. 1-2, p. 22.
32. Jones, p. 117. As early as the first part of 1948 IUS-WFDY delegations had been sent to Latin America. A Congress of Democratic Youth, which attacked U. S. and Western imperialism, was organized in Mexico City.
33. *Ibid.*, pp. 117-120.
34. *Youth and Freedom*, Vol. 3, No. 3-4, pp. 1-4.
35. *Ibid.*
36. *Borba* (Yugoslav Communist Party paper), August 18, 1960.

37. *News Features*, Vol. V, No. 3 (March 19, 1964), pp. 4-5.

38. *WFDY News*, No. 31, December 1962.

39. See *News Features*, Vol. IV, No. 7 (July 31, 1963), pp. 1-2, for a discussion of the splintering of the *Zengakuren* into five or six factions.

40. *WFDY News*, March 1963.

41. *News Features*, Vol. V, No. 3 (March 19, 1964), pp. 6-7.

42. *Tanjug* (Yugoslav news agency), February 28, 1960.

43. *MTI* (Hungarian news agency), August 8, 1963.

44. *Ibid.*, August 10, 1963.

45. *NCNA*, August 15, 1963.

46. *ADN* (East German news agency), August 31, 1963.

47. *Tanjug*, November 8, 1963.

48. *Mlady Svet* (Czechoslovak Communist youth paper), October 11, 1963.

49. *Antara* (Indonesian news agency), November 28, 1963.

50. NCNA, November 30 and December 13, 1963.

50. *Mladá Fronta* (Czechoslovak Communist youth paper), November 29, 1963.

52. NCNA, January 24, 25, and 27, 1964.

53. Djakarta Radio, January 25, 1964.

54. NCNA, January 30, 1964. It is interesting to note that the small, radical Puerto Rican student organization (FUPI) also has indicated its support for the new international youth organization. NCNA, March 30, 1964.

55. *Le Monde* (Paris), February 25, 1964.

56. *Ibid.*, February 20, 1964.

57. *News Features*, Vol. V, No. 3 (March 19, 1964), pp. 5, 7.

Youth Festivals: Their History and Function

1. Lamberz and Jeutner, p. 67.

2. *Background* (Washington; U. S. Department of State, Office of Public Affairs, September 1951), p. 7.

3. Vincent R. Tortora, *Communist Close-up* (New York: Exposition Press, 1954), pp. 75-77.

5. *Ibid.*, p. 44.

4. *World Youth*, Vol. 8, Special Edition, August 1953.

6. *Ibid.*, Vol. 10, No. 8-9 (August-September 1955), p. 1.

7. Compare the First Secretary of the Komsomol Central Com-

mittee, Alexander Shelepin, in *Komsomolskaya Pravda*, August 17, 1957, and *Molodoi Kommunist*, August 1957.

8. *VIIth World Festival of Youth and Students—Vienna 1959* (Prague: International Union of Students, 1959), p. 12.

9. *Komsomolskaya Pravda*, June 29, 1957.

10. *Courtship of Young Minds: A Case Study of the Moscow Youth Festival* (New York: East European Student and Youth Service, 1959), p. 14.

11. *Izvestia*, May 7, 1957.

12. *Komsomolskaya Pravda*, August 14, 1958.

13. *Festival* (newspaper of the International Preparatory Committee for the World Festivals of Youth and Students), No. 1 (Moscow Festival), September-October 1956, p. 1.

14. *Festival*, No. 1 (Warsaw), February 1-15, 1955, p. 2.

15. *The VIth World Festival of Youth and Students for Peace and Friendship* (n.p.: World Federation of Democratic Youth, 1957), p. 22.

16. See Morton Schwartz, "Moscow's Experimental Venture: The Vienna World Youth Festival," *Problems of Communism*, Vol. VIII, No. 6 (September-October 1959), pp. 53-56, for an observer's comments on the Vienna Festival; also *East Europe*, November 1959, pp. 22-23.

17. See Paul E. Sigmund, "Helsinki—The Last Youth Festival?" *Problems of Communism*, Vol. XI, No. 5 (September-October 1962), pp. 58-62, and *Youth and Freedom*, Vol. V, No. 4, for discussions of the Helsinki Festival.

(1945-1964)

1. *Ezhegodnik Bolshoi Sovetskoi Entsyklopedii*, 1963 (Annual Supplement to the Large Soviet Encyclopedia for 1963), p. 19.

2. Leo Gruliow and Charlotte Saikowski, *Current Soviet Policies: IV* (New York and London: Columbia University Press, 1962), p. 39.

3. From the report of S. P. Pavlov, First Secretary of the Komsomol Central Committee to the Fourteenth Komsomol Congress, *Pravda*, April 17, 1962 (*Current Digest of the Soviet Press*, Vol. XIV, No. 15, p. 1).

4. *Ibid.* (*Current Digest . . .*, pp. 5, 6).

5. *Ibid. (Current Digest . . ., p. 5).*

6. *Ibid. (Current Digest of the Soviet Press,* Vol. XIV, No. 16, p. 11).

7. *Ibid. (Current Digest . . .,* No. 16, p. 10).

8. *Ibid.*

9. See Fainsod, pp. 295-298.

10. *XIV S'ezd Vsesoiuznogo Leninskogo Kommunisticheskogo Soiuza Molodezhi, 16-20 Aprelia 1962 g. Stenograficheskii Otchet* (XIV Congress of the All-Union Leninist Communist Union of Youth, April 16-20, 1962. Stenographic Report) (Moscow: Molodaia Gvardiia, 1962), pp. 567-569.

11. S.P. Pavlov, born in 1929, has been First Secretary of the Komsomol since 1959, and has been active as a Komsomol functionary since 1952. He is at present a member of the Central Committee of the Communist Party of the Soviet Union, and if he follows in the footsteps of his two immediate predecessors he will eventually end up as head of the state security apparatus.

12. The Fourteenth Komsomol Congress approved a new statute that reduced the minimum age for Komsomol membership from fifteen to fourteen.

13. John N. Hazard, *The Soviet System of Government* (3d ed.; Chicago and London: University of Chicago Press, 1964), p. 40.

14. *Ezhegodnik . . . 1957,* p. 16.

15. *Pravda,* July 6, 1956 (*Current Digest of the Soviet Press,* Vol. VIII, No. 27, p. 37).

16. *Ezhegodnik . . . 1960,* p. 18.

17. *Ezhegodnik . . . 1957,* p. 16; *1963,* pp. 22-23.

18. *Ezhegodnik . . . 1963,* pp. 22-23.

19. See Richard F. Staar, "Regimentation of Youth in Satellite Poland," *The Southwestern Social Science Quarterly,* June 1956, pp. 7-19, and Richard F. Staar, *Poland, 1944-1962: The Sovietization of a Captive People* (Baton Rouge: Louisiana State University Press, 1962), Chapter 12, for a discussion of the youth and student movements in Poland in the period 1944-1962.

20. *Bolshaia Sovietskaia Entsyklopediia* (Large Soviet Encyclopedia) (2d ed.) Vol. 47, p. 316.

21. See Robert Finley Delaney (ed.), *This Is Communist Hungary* (Chicago: Regnery, 1958), pp. 166-167, 184; Ference A. Váli, *Rift and Revolt in Hungary* (Cambridge, Mass.: Harvard University Press, 1961), p. 43; Ernst C. Helmreich (ed.), *Hungary* (New York: Praeger, 1957), p. 128.

22. See Alex N. Dragnich, *Tito's Promised Land* (New Brunswick, N.J.: Rutgers University Press, 1954), pp. 133-134; *BSE*, Vol. 49, p. 338.

23. See Stephen Fischer-Galati (ed), *Romania* (New York and London: Atlantic Books, 1957), p. 78, and Alexandre Cretzianu (ed.), *Captive Rumania* (New York: Praeger, 1956), pp. 253-254.

24. See L.A.D. Dellin (ed.), *Bulgaria* (New York: Praeger, 1957), p. 161.

25. See Stavro Skendi (ed.), *Albania* (London: Atlantic Press, 1957), pp. 87-88.

26. See Kuo-chön, Chao, *The Mass Organizations in Communist China* (Cambridge, Mass.: Center for International Studies, Massachusetts Institute of Technology, 1953), pp. 62-83, for the development of the Chinese youth organization.

27. See *International Jugendkorrespondenz*, June 10, 1920; June 1, 1921, pp. 6-7; November 30, 1921, pp. 4-5; and October 15, 1922 for the early efforts by the Soviet youth organization to assist in the formation of a Chinese Communist youth organization.

28. *Youth and Freedom*, Vol. VI, No. 1-2, p. 17: Vol. III, No. 5-6, p. 17.

29. *BSE*, Vol. 22, p. 611.

30. VNA (North Vietnamese news agency), March 21 and 25, 1961.

31. See Henry J. Kellermann, *The Present Status of German Youth* (Washington: U.S. Department of State, 1946; 25 pp.); Friedrich, *op. cit.*; and *German Youth Between Yesterday and Tomorrow* (Berlin: U.S. Office of Military Government for Germany, 1948; 36 pp.) for the activities of the Soviet authorities in organizing the youth after the war.

32. Gerd Friedrich, *Die Freie Deutsche Jugend* (The Free German Youth), (Cologne: Rote Weissbücher, 1950), p. 21.
33. *Ibid.*, pp. 26-29.
34. *Ibid.*
35. *Ibid.*, p. 51.
36. See James W. Miller, "Youth in Dictatorships," *American Political Science Review*, October 1938, pp. 965-970, and Eric Josephson, "Political Youth Organizations in Europe, 1900-1950" (Unpublished Ph.D. dissertation, Columbia University, 1959).
37. Friedrich, p. 14.
38. See "Hungarian Youth in Revolt," *East Europe*, January 1957, pp. 26-27; "Children of the Revolution," *East Europe*, November 1962, pp. 2-10.
39. MTI (Hungarian news agency), May 12, 1958.
40. "Crisis in the Youth Leagues," *News From Behind the Iron Curtain*, June 1955, pp. 25-35.
41. *Youth and Freedom*, Vol. V, No. 1-2, p. 13.
42. *Ibid.*

Today and Tomorrow

1. See *Komsomolskaya Pravda*, February 28, 1957, for the decree of the Komsomol Central Committee on ideological training of the youth.
2. *Ibid.*, p. 13.
3. Great Britain, France, West Germany, and other Western countries have also concluded cultural exchange agreements with the Soviet Union.
4. From the report of S. P. Pavlov, First Secretary of the Komsomol Central Committee, to the Fourteenth Komsomol Congress, *Pravda* and *Izvestia*, April 17, 1962 (*Current Digest of the* Soviet Press, Vol. XIV, No. 16, p. 7.).
5. *Ibid.* (*Current Digest . . .*, p. 10).

Selected Bibliography

This bibliography includes the main sources on the international Communist youth movement available in English, and a number of important works on international Communism in general. In addition, there are included certain works in German and Russian that one who reads these languages will find most useful. For more detailed references on specific points, see the foreign-language sources cited in the footnotes in the text.

Afonin, A. *A Short History of the Young Communist League of the Soviet Union.* Moscow-Leningrad: Cooperative Publishing Society of Foreign Workers in the U.S.S.R., 1934.

Apeland, Nils. *World Youth and the Communists.* London: Phoenix House, 1958.

Background. Washington, D. C.: U. S. Department of State, Office of Public Affairs, September 1951.

The Background of the 7th World Youth Festival. Report prepared by the Independent Service for Information on the Vienna Youth Festival. Cambridge, Mass.: Independent Service for the Vienna Youth Festival, 1959.

Blumenau, Ralph. *Communists and Students.* London: Batchworth Press, 1954.

Bolshaia Sovietskaia Entsyklopediia (Large Soviet Encyclopedia). 2d. ed.

Borkenau, Franz. *European Communism*. London: Faber & Faber, 1953.

————. *World Communism*. Ann Arbor, Mich.: University of Michigan Press (Ann Arbor Paperbacks), 1962.

Bulletin of the Student Needs and Welfare Department of the IUS (International Union of Students), Prague. Published irregularly.

Chemadanov, V. *We Are For the United Front*. New York: Youth Publishers, 1934.

————. *Young Communists and the Path to Soviet Power*. New York: Youth Publishers, 1934.

Clarity (theoretical organ of the Young Communist League, U.S.A.). Bimonthly.

Clews, John. "Communism's Fourth Lever: The Youth and Student Fronts," *Problems of Communism*, Vol. V (1956), No. 6, pp. 39-44.

Courtship of Young Minds: A Case Study of the Moscow Youth Festival. New York: East European Student and Youth Service, 1959.

Cretzianu, Alexandre (ed.). *Captive Romania*. New York: Praeger, 1956.

The Day Is Ours! Report of Comrade M. Woolf to the 6th World Congress of the Young Communist International. London: Young Communist International, 1935.

Dellin, L.A.D. (ed.). *Bulgaria*. New York: Praeger, 1957.

Die sogenannten Weltjugendfestspiele im Sowjetsektor von Berlin (The So-Called World Youth Festival in the Soviet Sector of Berlin). Bonn: Federal Ministry for All-German Affairs, 1951.

Dragnich, Alex N. *Tito's Promised Land*. New Brunswick, N. J.: Rutgers University Press, 1954.

East Europe. Published monthly by the Free Europe Committee; previously titled *News From Behind the Iron Curtain*.

Fainsod, Merle. *How Russia Is Ruled*. Rev. ed. Cambridge, Mass.: Harvard University Press, 1963.

Festival. Newspaper of the International Preparatory Committee for the World Festivals of Youth and Students. Published irregularly.

Festival News. Published by the East European Studens and Youth Service (June-December 1957).

Fischer-Galati, Stephen (ed.). *Romania.* New York: Atlantic Books, 1957.

Fisher, Ralph. *Pattern for Soviet Youth.* New York: Columbia University Press, 1959.

Friedrich, Gerd. *Die Freie Deutsche Jugend* (The Free German Youth). Cologne: Rote Weissbücher, 1950.

German Youth Between Yesterday and Tomorrow. Berlin: U. S. Office of Military Government for Germany, 1948.

Green, Gil. *Facing the 8th Convention of the Young Communist League. Report to the National Conference of the Young Communist League delivered January 1, 1937.* New York: National Committee, Young Communist League, 1937.

Gruliow, Leo (ed.). *Current Soviet Policies.* New York: Praeger, 1953.

———. *Current Soviet Policies: II.* New York: Praeger, 1957.

———. *Current Soviet Policies: III.* New York: Columbia University Press, 1960.

Gruliow, Leo, and Saikowski, Charlotte. *Current Soviet Policies: IV.* New York and London: Columbia University Press, 1962.

Hazard, John N. *The Soviet System of Government.* 3d. ed. Chicago and London: University of Chicago Press, 1964.

Helmreich, Ernst C. (ed.). *Hungary.* New York: Praeger, 1957.

Institute for the Study of the U.S.S.R. *Soviet Youth: Twelve Komsomol Histories.* (Series I, No. 51.) Munich: The Institute, 1959.

———. *Youth in Ferment.* (Series I, No. 66.) Munich: The Institute, 1962.

———. *Youth in the Soviet Union.* (Series I, No. 53.) Munich: The Institute, 1959.

International of Youth. Organ of the Executive Committee of the Communist Youth International. Published in London and New York; Russian edition is *Internatsional Molodezhi.*

International Press Correspondence. Published weekly by the

Executive Committee of the Communist International; title changed in 1938 to *World News and Views.*

International Union of Students. *Executive Committee Meeting. Vienna. 19-21 January 1954.* Prague: International Union of Students, 1954.

International Union of Students, IX Annual Council Meeting, Moscow. 20-27 August 1954. Prague: International Union of Students, 1954.

International Union of Students. *Executive Committee Meeting, Prague. March 1955.* Prague: International Union of Students, 1955.

IUS Calendar of Activities in the Field of Culture and Sport for 1952. Prague: International Union of Students, 1952.

Jones, Peter T. *The History of U. S. National Student Association Relations with the International Union of Students, 1945-1956.* Philadelphia: Foreign Policy Research Institute, University of Pennsylvania, 1956.

Juviler, Peter. "Communist Morality and Soviet Youth," *Problems of Communism,* May-June 1961.

Kassof, Allen. "Afflictions of the Youth League," *Problems of Communism,* Vol. VII (1958), No. 5, pp. 17-23.

————. "Youth vs. the Regime: Conflict in Values," *Problems of Communism,* Vol. VI (1957), No. 3, pp. 15-23.

Kellermann, Henry J. *The Present Status of German Youth.* Washington: U. S. Department of State, 1946.

KPSS o komsomole i molodezhi (The CPSU on the Komsomol and the Youth). Moscow: Molodaia Gvardiia, 1957.

Kuo-chün, Chao. *The Mass Organizations in Communist China.* Cambridge, Mass.: Center for International Studies, Massachusetts Institute of Technology, 1953.

Lamberz, Werner, and Jeutner, Klaus. *Vereint mit 87 Millionen* (United with 87 Million). East Berlin: Verlag Neues Leben, 1960.

Laski, Harold. "Students and Politics," *The Nation,* December 21, 1946, pp. 227-228.

Lenin, V. I. *An die Jugend. Reden und Aufsätze* (To the Youth. Speeches and Articles). Vienna: Verlag der Kommunistischen Jugend-Internationale, 1925.

Vsemirnyi Festival Molodezhi v Prage (World Festival of Youth in Prague). Prague: Orbis, 1948.

Weiss, Max. *One Issue, One Enemy, One War; Destroy Hitlerism.* New York: New Age Publishers, 1941.

What Is New in the Student Movement? How Can Unity be Achieved? Prague: International Union of Students, 1956.

Why the IUS Has Severed Relations with the Leaders of the Student Section of the "People's Youth of Yugoslavia." Prague: International Union of Students, 1950.

Working Class Unity—Bulwark Against Fascism: Report by Dimitrov at the Seventh Comintern Congress. New York: Workers' Library Publishers, 1935.

World Student News. Monthly of the International Union of Students.

World Youth. Monthly of the World Federation of Democratic Youth.

The Young Communist International between the Fourth and Fifth Congresses, 1924-28. London: Communist Party of Great Britain, 1928.

Youth Demands a Peaceful World. Report of the Second World Youth Congress, Vassar College, Poughkeepsie, New York, August 16-23, 1938. New York: World Youth Congress, 1938.

Youth Fights for Peace, Jobs, Civil Rights (Reports to the National Council of the Young Communist League of the United States, New York, May 1940). New York: New Age Publishers, 1940.

Youth and Freedom. Published by the Institute for International Youth Affairs, New York.

Youth Plans a New World; Being the Official Record of the First World Youth Congress (Geneva, 31 August-6 September, 1936). Geneva: International Federation of League of Nations Societies, 1936.

Index